SCHOLA

DECEMBER
Monthly Idea Book

Ready-to-Use Templates, Activities, Management Tools, and More — for Every Day of the Month

Karen Sevaly

New York • Toronto • London • Auckland • Sydney **Teaching**
Mexico City • New Delhi • Hong Kong • Buenos Aires *Resources*

DEDICATION
This book is dedicated to teachers and children everywhere.

Cover design by Maria Lilja
Cover art by Jillian Phillips
Interior design by Holly Grundon
Illustrations by Karen Sevaly

ISBN 978-0-545-37936-6

Text and illustrations © 2013 by Scholastic Inc.
All rights reserved.
Printed in the U.S.A.

2 3 4 5 6 7 8 9 10   40   19 18 17 16 15 14

CONTENTS

FAVORITE TOPICS

CONTENTS

FUN & FESTIVE!

Reproducible Patterns

HANUKKAH: THE FESTIVAL OF LIGHTS

CHRISTMAS AROUND THE WORLD

CONTENTS

KWANZAA: A CULTURAL CELEBRATION

AWARDS, INCENTIVES, AND MORE

ANSWER KEY

INTRODUCTION

Welcome to the original Monthly Idea Book series! This book was written especially for teachers getting ready to teach topics related to the month of December.

Each book in this month-by-month series is filled with dozens of ideas for PreK–3 classrooms. Activities connect to the Common Core State Standards for Reading (Foundational Skills), among other subjects, to help you meet the needs of your students. (For more information, see page 16.)

Most everything you need to prepare the lessons and activities in this resource is included, such as:

- calendar and weather-related props

- book cover patterns and stationery for writing assignments

- booklet patterns

- games and puzzles that support learning in curriculum areas such as math, science, and writing

- activity sheets that help students organize information, respond to learning, and explore topics in a meaningful way

- patterns for projects that connect to holidays, special occasions, and commemorative events

All year long, you can weave the ideas and reproducible patterns in these unique books into your monthly lesson plans and classroom activities. Happy teaching!

What's Inside

You'll find that this book is chockfull of reproducibles that make lesson planning easier:

- ■ puppets and
  picture props

- ■ bookmarks, booklets,
  and book covers

- ■ game boards, puzzles,
  and word finds

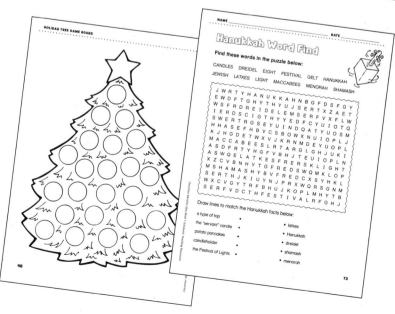

■ greeting cards
and stationery

■ awards and certificates

How to Use This Book

The reproducible pages in this book have flexible use and may be modified to meet your particular classroom needs. Use the reproducible activity pages and patterns in conjunction with the suggested activities provided or weave them into your curriculum in other ways.

★ PHOTOCOPY OR SCAN

To get started, think about your developing lesson plans and upcoming bulletin boards. If desired, carefully remove the pages you will need. Duplicate those pages on copy paper, color paper, tagboard, or overhead transparency sheets. If you have access to a scanner, consider saving the pattern pages as PDF files. That way you can size images up or down and customize them with text to create individualized lessons, center-time activities, interactive whiteboard lessons, homework pages, and more.

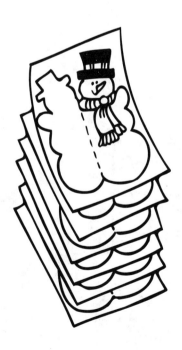

★ LAMINATE FOR DURABILITY

Laminating the reproducibles will help you extend their use. If you have access to a roll laminator, then you already know how fortunate you are when it comes to saving time and resources. If you don't have a laminator, clear adhesive vinyl covering works well. Just sandwich the pattern between two sheets of vinyl and cut off any excess. Then try some of these ideas:

- Put laminated sheets of stationery in a writing center to use for handwriting practice. Wipe-off markers work great on coated pages and can easily be erased with dry tissue.

- Add longevity to calendars, weather-related pictures, and pocket chart rebus pictures by preserving them with lamination.

- Transform picture props into flannel board figures. After lamination, add a tab of hook-and-loop fastener to the back of the props and invite students to adhere them to the flannel board for storytelling fun.

- To enliven magnet board activities, affix sections of magnet tape to the back of picture props. Then encourage students to sort images according to the skills you're working on. For example, you might have them group images by commonalities such as initial sound, habitat, or physical attributes.

★ BULLETIN BOARDS

1. Set the Stage

Use background paper colors that complement many themes and seasons. For example, the dark background you use as a spooky display in October will have dramatic effect in November, when you begin a unit on woodland animals or Thanksgiving.

While paper works well, there are other background options available. You might also try fabric from a colorful bed sheet or gingham material. Discontinued rolls of patterned wallpaper can be purchased at discount stores. What's more, newspapers are easy to use and readily available. Attach a background of comics to set off a lesson on riddles, or use grocery store flyers to provide food for thought on a bulletin board about nutrition.

2. Make the Display

The reproducible patterns in this book can be enlarged to fit your needs. When we say enlarge, we mean it! Think BIG! Use an overhead projector to enlarge the images you need to make your bulletin board extraordinary.

If your school has a stencil press, you're lucky. The rest of us can use these strategies for making headers and titles.

- Cut strips of paper, cloud shapes, or cartoon bubbles. They will all look great! Then, by hand, write the text using wide-tipped permanent markers or tempera paint.

- If you must cut individual letters, use 4- by 6-inch pieces of construction paper. (Laminate first, if you can.) Cut the uppercase letters as shown on page 14. No need to measure, as somewhat irregular letters will look creative, not messy.

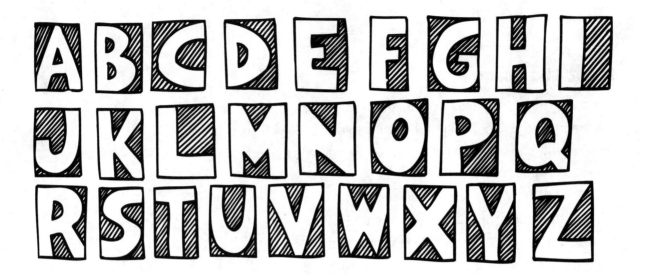

3. Add Color and Embellishments

Use your imagination! You'll be surprised at the great displays you can create.

■ Watercolor markers work great on small areas. On larger areas, you can switch to crayons, color chalk, or pastels. (Lamination will keep the color off of you. No laminator? A little hairspray will do the trick as a fixative.)

■ Cut character eyes and teeth from white paper and glue them in place. The features will really stand out and make your bulletin boards engaging.

■ For special effects, include items that provide texture and visual interest, such as buttons, yarn, and lace. Try cellophane or blue glitter glue on water scenes. Consider using metallic wrapping paper or aluminum foil to add a bit of shimmer to stars and belt buckles.

■ Finally, take a picture of your completed bulletin board. Store the photos in a recipe box or large sturdy envelope. Next year when you want to create the same display, you'll know right where everything goes. You might even want to supply students with pushpins and invite them to recreate the display, following your directions and using the photograph as support.

Staying Organized

Organizing materials with monthly file folders provides
you with a location to save reproducible activity pages and
patterns, along with related craft ideas, recipes, and magazine
or periodical articles.

If you prefer, use file boxes instead of folders. You'll find
that with boxes there will plenty of room to store enlarged
patterns, sample art projects, bulletin board materials, and
much more.

Meeting the Standards

CONNECTIONS TO THE COMMON CORE STATE STANDARDS

The Common Core State Standards Initiative (CCSSI) has outlined learning expectations in English/Language Arts, among other subject areas, for students at different grade levels. In general, the activities in this book align with the following standards for students in grades K–3. For more information, visit the CCSSI website at www.corestandards.org.

Reading: Foundational Skills

Print Concepts
- RF.K.1, RF.1.1. Demonstrate understanding of the organization and basic features of print.

Phonics and Word Recognition
- RF.K.3, RF.1.3, RF.2.3, RF.3.3. Know and apply grade-level phonics and word analysis skills in decoding words.

Fluency
- RF.K.4. Read emergent-reader texts with purpose and understanding.
- RF.1.4, RF.2.4, RF.3.4. Read with sufficient accuracy and fluency to support comprehension.

Writing

Production and Distribution of Writing
- W.3.4. Produce writing in which the development and organization are appropriate to task and purpose.
- W.K.5, W.1.5, W.2.5, W.3.5. Focus on a topic and strengthen writing as needed by revising and editing.

Research to Build and Present Knowledge
- W.K.7, W.1.7, W.2.7. Participate in shared research and writing projects.
- W.3.7. Conduct short research projects that build knowledge about a topic.
- W.K.8, W.1.8, W.2.8, W.3.8. Recall information from experiences or gather information from provided sources to answer a question.

Range of Writing
- W.3.10. Write routinely over extended time frames (time for research, reflection, and revision) and shorter time frames (a single sitting or a day or two) for a range of discipline-specific tasks, purposes, and audiences.

Speaking & Listening

Comprehension and Collaboration
- SL.K.1, SL.1.1, SL.2.1. Participate in collaborative conversations with diverse partners about grade-level topics and texts with peers and adults in small and larger groups.
- SL.K.2, SL.1.2, SL.2.2, SL.3.2. Recount or describe key ideas or details from a text read aloud or information presented orally or through other media.
- SL.K.3, SL.1.3, SL.2.3, SL.3.3. Ask and answer questions about what a speaker says in order to gather additional information or clarify something that is not understood.

Presentation of Knowledge and Ideas
- SL.K.4, SL.1.4, SL.2.4. Describe people, places, things, and events with relevant details, expressing ideas and feelings clearly.
- SL.K.5, SL.1.5, SL.2.5, SL.3.5. Add drawings or other visual displays to stories or recounts of experiences when appropriate to clarify ideas, thoughts, and feelings.

Language

Conventions of Standard English
- L.K.1, L.1.1, L.2.1, L.3.1. Demonstrate command of the conventions of standard English grammar and usage when writing or speaking.
- L.K.2, L.1.2, L.2.2, L.3.2. Demonstrate command of the conventions of standard English capitalization, punctuation, and spelling when writing.

Knowledge of Language
- L.2.3, L.3.3. Use knowledge of language and its conventions when writing, speaking, reading, or listening.

Vocabulary Acquisition and Use
- L.K.4, L.1.4, L.2.4, L.3.4. Determine or clarify the meaning of unknown and multiple-meaning words and phrases based on grade level reading and content, choosing flexibly from an array of strategies.
- L.K.6, L.1.6, L.2.6, L.3.6. Use words and phrases acquired through conversations, reading and being read to, and responding to texts.

CALENDAR TIME

Getting Started

			December			
Sunday	Monday	Tuesday	Wednesday	Thursday	Friday	Saturday

19

CALENDAR

★ MARK YOUR CALENDAR

Make photocopies of the calendar grid on page 19 and use it to meet your needs. Consider using the write-on spaces to:

- write the corresponding numerals for each day

- mark and count how many days have passed

- track the weather with stamps or stickers

- note student birthdays

- record homework assignments

- communicate with families about positive behaviors

- remind volunteers about schedules, field trips, shortened days, and so on

CELEBRATIONS THIS MONTH

Whether you post a photocopy of pages 20 through 23 near your class calendar or just turn to these pages for inspiration, you're sure to find lots of information on them to discuss with students. To take celebrating and learning a step further, invite the class to add more to the list. For example, students can add anniversaries of significant events and the birthdays of their favorite authors or historical figures.

CALENDAR HEADER

You can make a photocopy of the header on page 24, color it, and use it as a title for your classroom calendar. You might opt to give the coloring job to a student who has a birthday that month. The student is sure to enjoy seeing his or her artwork each and every day of the month.

BEFORE INTRODUCING WHAT'S THE WEATHER?

Make a photocopy of the body template on page 25. Laminate it so you can use it again and again. Before sharing the template with the class, cut out pieces of cloth in the shapes of clothing students typically wear this month. For example, if you live in a warm weather climate, your December attire might include shorts and t-shirts. If you live in chillier climates, your attire might include a scarf, hat, and coat. Fit the cutouts to the body outline. When the clothing props are made, and you're ready to have students dress the template, display the clothing. Invite the "weather helper of the day" to tell what pieces of clothing he or she would choose to dress appropriately for the weather. (For extra fun, use foam to cut out accessories such as an umbrella, sunhat, and raincoat.)

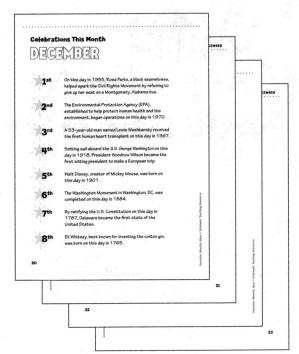

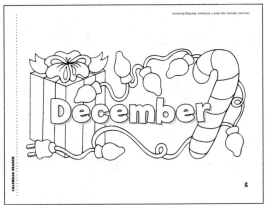

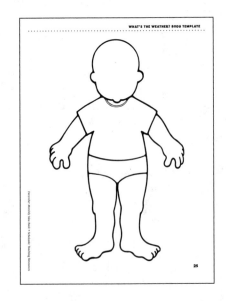

December

Sunday	Monday	Tuesday	Wednesday	Thursday	Friday	Saturday

Celebrations This Month

DECEMBER

1st On this day in 1955, Rosa Parks, a black seamstress, helped spark the Civil Rights Movement by refusing to give up her seat on a Montgomery, Alabama bus.

2nd The Environmental Protection Agency (EPA), established to help protect human health and the environment, began operations on this day in 1970.

3rd A 53-year-old man named Lewis Washkansky received the first human heart transplant on this day in 1967.

4th Setting sail aboard the *S.S. George Washington* on this day in 1918, President Woodrow Wilson became the first sitting president to make a European trip.

5th Walt Disney, creator of Mickey Mouse, was born on this day in 1901.

6th The Washington Monument in Washington, DC, was completed on this day in 1884.

7th By ratifying the U.S. Constitution on this day in 1787, Delaware became the first state of the United States.

8th Eli Whitney, best known for inventing the cotton gin, was born on this day in 1765.

December Monthly Idea Book © Scholastic Teaching Resources

9th The famous American clown Emmett Kelly, who created the hobo clown known as "Weary Willie," was born on this day in 1898.

10th On this day in 1901, the first Nobel Prizes were awarded in Sweden in the fields of chemistry, literature, medicine, physics, and peace.

11th The United Nations International Children's Emergency Fund (UNICEF) was established on this day in 1946 to provide food and healthcare to children in countries that had been devastated in World War II.

12th Guglielmo Marconi sent the first radio transmission across the Atlantic Ocean on this day in 1901. The message traveled from Cornwall, England to Newfoundland, Canada.

13th Today in Sweden, people celebrate Saint Lucia's Day with a special candlelight procession led by a girl crowned to portray Lucia.

14th On this day in 1911, Norwegian Roald Amundsen became the first explorer to reach the South Pole.

15th The first ten amendments to the U. S. Constitution, called the Bill of Rights, became law on this day in 1791.

16th On this day in 1773, a group of American colonists dumped British tea in the Boston Harbor. This event is now known as the "Boston Tea Party."

17th Brothers Orville and Wilbur Wright made the first successful flight of a self-propelled airplane on this day in 1903. The plane traveled 120 feet, staying aloft for 12 seconds.

18th On this day in 1620, the *Mayflower*, carrying 102 passengers, docked at Plymouth Harbor in Massachussetts, while a survey team set out to search for a settlement site.

19th *Apollo 17* completed the last lunar-landing mission on this date in 1972. During the mission, the astronauts spent 75 hours exploring the surface of the moon.

20th As part of the land acquisition agreement known as the Louisiana Purchase, France turned New Orleans over to the United States on this day in 1803.

21st On this day in 1937, Walt Disney's first feature-length animated movie, *Snow White and the Seven Dwarfs*, premiered to a record-breaking audience.

22nd Today is the birth date of Colo, the first gorilla to be born in captivity. Colo was born in 1956 at the Columbus Zoo in Ohio.

23rd George Washington resigned as Commander-in-Chief of the Continental Army on this day in 1783. A few years later, Washington was elected the first President of the United States.

December Monthly Idea Book © Scholastic Teaching Resources

24th On this day in 1923, President Calvin Coolidge lit the first national Christmas tree at the White House. The tree was also the first to be decorated with electric lights.

25th Today, people around the world celebrate Christmas.

26th In 1966, the first day of the very first Kwanzaa, a seven-day holiday rooted in African heritage, was observed on this day in Los Angeles, California.

27th The famous French chemist Louis Pasteur was born on this day in 1822.

28th On this day in 1869, a dentist named William Semple became one of the first persons to patent chewing gum.

29th This date marks the anniversary of the opening of Radio City Music Hall in New York City. The Hall first opened its doors in 1932 and was the largest indoor theatre in the world.

30th On this day in 1963, Congress authorized minting a new half dollar in tribute to assassinated president John F. Kennedy. The coin replaced the Franklin half dollar.

31st Today is New Year's Eve!

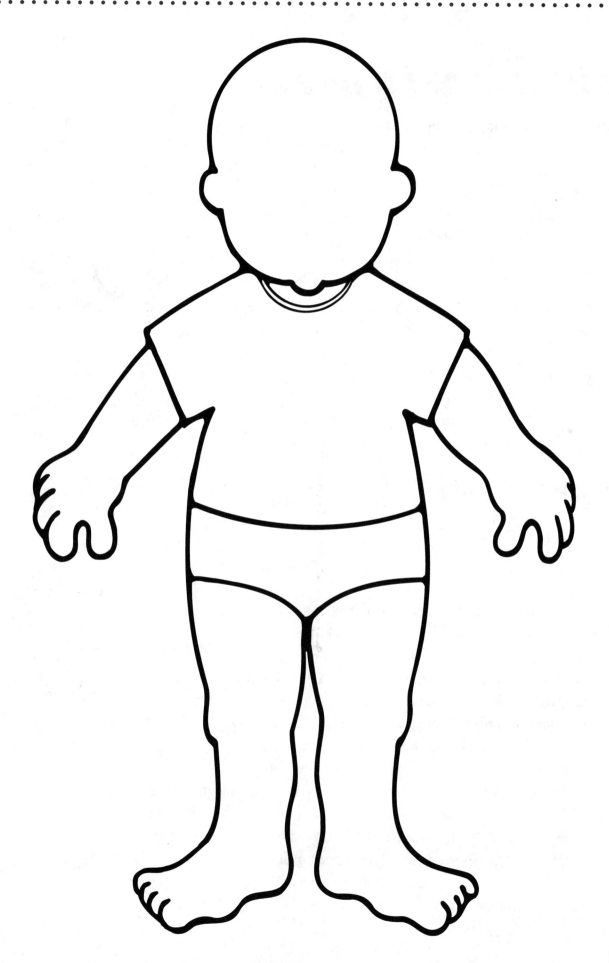

GINGERBREAD DAYS!

Throughout England and many other European countries, gingerbread and gingerbread cookies are a family tradition. Shopkeepers and market vendors often sell these delicious ginger-spiced cakes, cookies, and breads, which are commonly cut into various shapes and symbols that reflect the season. In some areas, towns hold Gingerbread Fairs where townspeople compete in making gingerbread houses and cookies.

   In the United States, gingerbread cookies have become popular winter holiday treats. Early settlers brought the custom of making gingerbread recipes to colonial America. As the country has grown, so has the tradition, along with making cookies in the shape of holiday symbols and constructing gingerbread houses. In fact, some towns—such as Lahaska, Pennsylvania—celebrate the Christmas holiday with a Gingerbread House Competition, in which numerous cash prizes are given to the most elaborately decorated gingerbread houses.

Suggested Activities

★ YUMMY TREAT

Gingerbread men are fun to make and so good to eat! Invite your class to make a batch of gingerbread men cookies to kick off this unit. First, gather a supply of gingerbread men cookie cutters. Or, have students make their own cookie-cutter templates from the pattern on page 30. For the templates, have students cut out tagboard copies of the pattern. Then make the cookie dough by following the directions on a package of gingerbread cookie mix. (Use as many packages as needed so that you have enough dough for each student to make a cookie.) Roll out the dough

onto waxed paper, then invite students to cut out their gingerbread men. If using the tagboard templates, have them cut around the shape with a plastic knife that has a smooth, rounded blade (not serrated). Students can then add raisin facial features to their gingerbread men. After the cookies have been baked and cooled, students can use icing and small candies to create additional features, such as hair, a collar, sleeve cuffs, and buttons.

★ SCENTED ORNAMENTS

Invite students to make scented gingerbread men ornaments to take home and enjoy with their families. Simply have them cut out a photocopy of the template on page 30, trace it onto brown construction paper or a heavy grocery bag, then cut out the shape. Students can use white poster paint, glitter crayons, or colored markers to decorate their cutouts. To add scent, have students trace the edge of their cutout with a glue stick and sprinkle a light layer of cinnamon powder onto the glue. To complete, help them attach a loop of yarn to the top of their gingerbread man to create a hanger.

★ GINGERBREAD MAN TALE

Share the traditional tale of the Gingerbread Man with students. Then invite them to make one of the puppets described below to use in retellings of the story. You might retell the story, having students move their puppets and recite the Gingerbread Man's chant each time he speaks. Or, encourage students to retell the story in their own words, using their puppets as props.

Stick Puppet

Distribute photocopies of the gingerbread man pattern on page 31. (You might copy the pattern onto tagboard or sturdy paper.) Instruct students to color their pattern and cut it out. If desired, they might use craft items to further embellish their cutout, such as using real buttons and ribbon trim on their gingerbread man's body. Finally, have them glue a wide craft-stick handle to the back of their puppet.

Hinged Gingerbread Man

Photocopy and distribute the gingerbread man patterns (pages 32–33) to students. Ask students to color and cut out their patterns, then use craft items to add embellishments to the pieces. Next, have them use five brass fasteners to attach the head, arms, and legs to the body where indicated. If desired, invite students to glue a wide craft stick to the back of their gingerbread man's body to use as a puppet handle. They can move their puppet in a variety of ways to make it dance or to spin and wiggle its limbs in amusing ways. To reinforce good behavior or reward completing assignments, you might award one part of the gingerbread puppet at a time to students when they meet an established goal. Once a student has collected all six pieces, he or she can then assemble the puppet.

★ GINGERBREAD MAN STORY PROPS

Encourage students to tap into their creativity as they retell the story of the Gingerbread Man, or make up their own versions of the tale. To prepare props for this activity, make tagboard photocopies of the pictures on pages 34 through 37. Color, cut out, and laminate the gingerbread man, animals, and barn. Then attach hook-and-loop fasteners to the back of each image for use with a flannelboard. Or, affix adhesive magnet strips to the pieces for use with a magnet board. Finally, invite individuals, pairs, or small groups to use the props to tell their stories.

★ GINGERBREAD MAN TWIST

Invite students to write "yummy" gingerbread-related stories, songs, poems, skits, or other creative writing activities, such as recipes or cheers. When finished, distribute photocopies of the book cover on page 38. Have students color and cut out their cover, add a title and author line, then glue it to a folded sheet of construction paper, aligning the straight edge along the fold where indicated. Then help them staple their written work inside the cover. Later, encourage students to share their books with the class. Alternately, students might use the book cover pattern to create holiday cards for friends or family members.

Following are some suggestions and "twists" students might consider including in their written work:

- ■ Retell the story featuring animals from a different habitat, such as a rainforest or desert.

- ■ Include humorous events, such as having the Gingerbread Man pause to ask the cow to "Moo-oove!" or do a somersault as he goes over a fence.

- ■ Write about a gingerbread dog, elephant, whale, or other animal.

- ■ Create an alternate setting, such as the moon, an isolated island, or Antarctica.

- ■ Make up a gingerbread recipe that can be used to feed a giant.

- ■ Write a poem, song, or rhyme about dancing gingerbread characters.

★ GINGERBREAD HOUSE

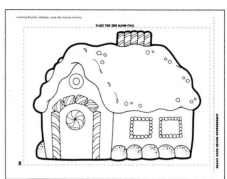

Work together with students to make a class gingerbread house. You might purchase a kit that includes all of the ingredients needed to build the house, or bring in the ingredients of your choice. Or, provide enough ingredients for partners to make gingerbread houses. (The complexity or simplicity of the project will be up to you and your students.) When finished, display the house(s) and discuss with students the steps they followed to create the project. Finally, use students' experiences as inspiration for them to create stories about a gingerbread house. They can write realistic or imaginary stories about how the house was built, who built it, the inhabitants of the house, and so on. If desired, collect students' completed stories to compile into a class book. You can use a photocopy of page 39 to create a cover for the book. Title the cover, add your class name, and invite a few volunteers to color the art. Then bind the pages to the cover and place the book in your class library for students to enjoy.

★ GINGERBREAD HOUSE GREETING CARD

Invite students to create a gingerbread-house card to send seasonal greetings to a friend or loved one. First, photocopy a supply of the card pattern (page 40) onto construction paper. Have children cut out the card, write their message on the back, and sign their name. They might also include a seasonal illustration. Then instruct them to color the front of card. Afterward, have students fold the card back along the dotted lines so that the two edges meet at the center and cover the text on the back. For a final touch, invite students to scent their gingerbread-house cards by gently rubbing a cinnamon stick over the front.

★ GINGERBREAD FLASH CARDS

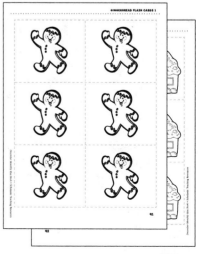

Reinforce whatever your students are learning with flash cards that fit the theme of this unit. Simply photocopy the cards on pages 41 and 42 and cut them apart. You can program the back of the cards for use as flash cards to teach letters and numbers, math facts, content-area vocabulary words, sight words, and so on. The cards are ideal for learning-center activities, but you might also use them to label job charts, group students, and more. To store, just put them in a resealable plastic bag.

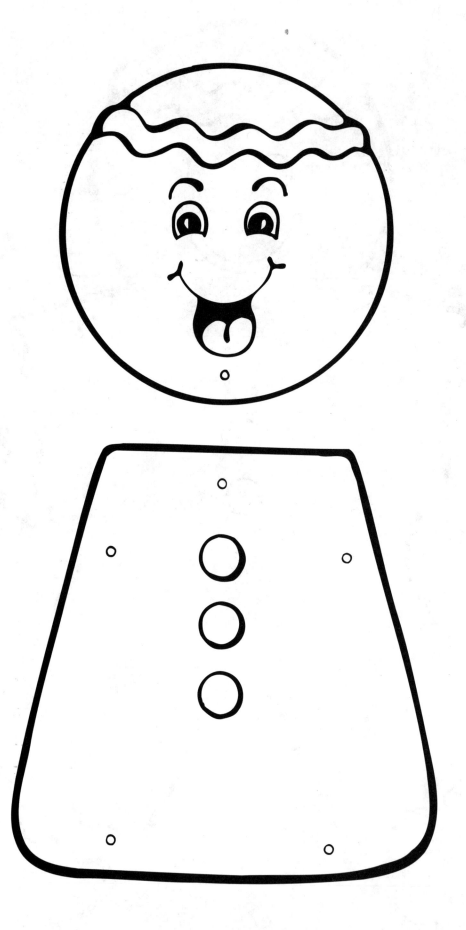

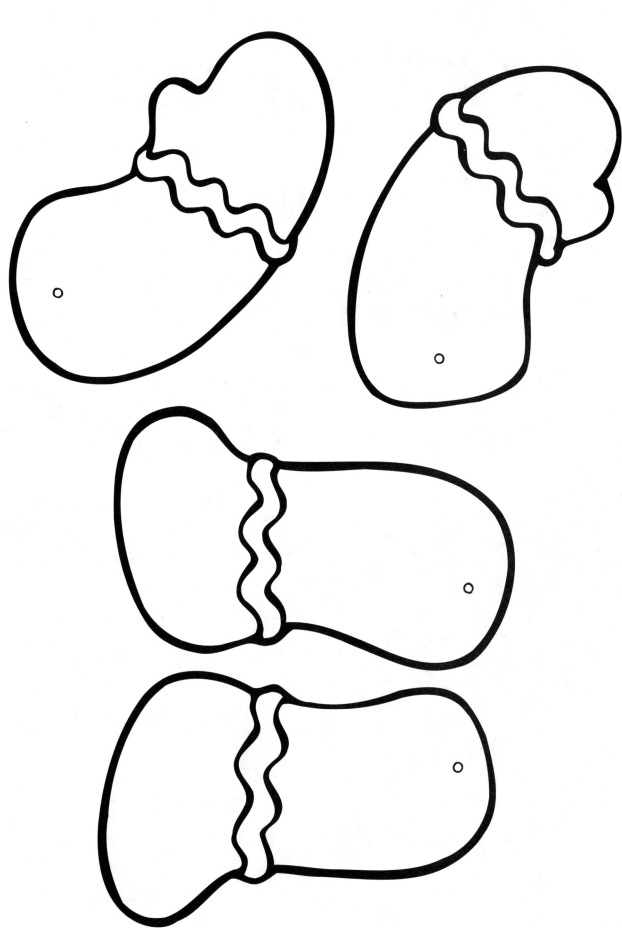

PLACE THIS SIDE ALONG FOLD.

December Monthly Idea Book © Scholastic Teaching Resources

PLACE THIS SIDE ALONG FOLD.

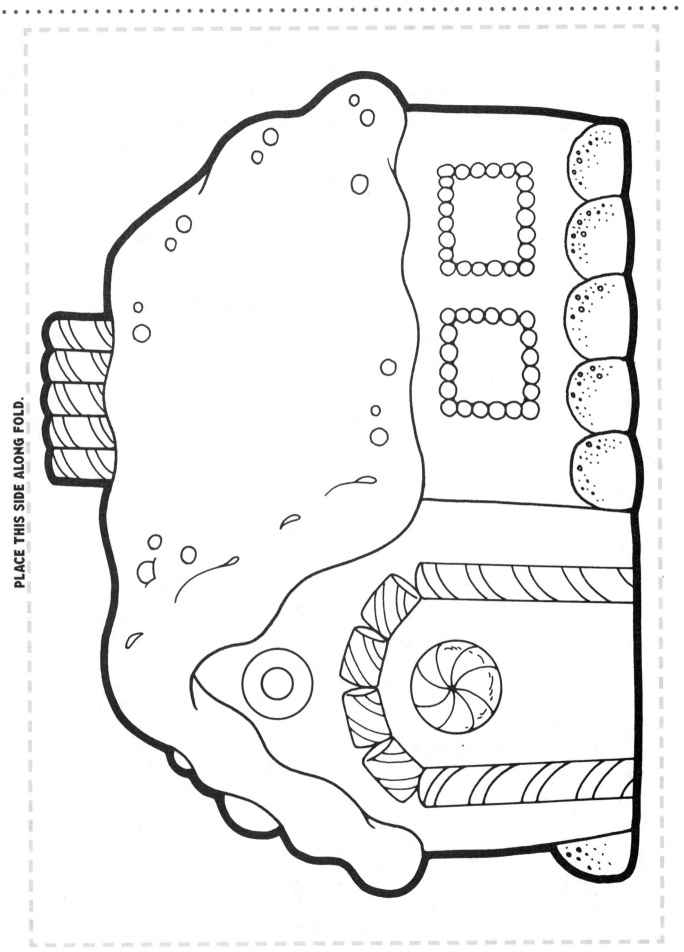

Happy Holidays

December Monthly Idea Book © Scholastic Teaching Resources

FUN & FESTIVE!

The month of December is filled with many exciting events. The first day of winter occurs during this month, and numerous cultures around the world celebrate special holidays, such as Hanukkah, Las Posadas, Christmas, and Kwanzaa. These celebrations are often occasions of festive gatherings and fun activities. In this unit, you'll find a treasure trove of seasonal-themed projects and activities that help reinforce skills across the curriculum.

Suggested Activities

★ DECORATE THE HOLIDAY TREE!

This open-ended game can be used in a variety of ways to teach or reinforce skills. To prepare, photocopy page 48 on light green paper. (Or use an overhead projector to make a large version of the tree.) If desired, cut out the tree. Then, to prepare the game for two players or teams, cut out two sets of round markers, making each set a different color and sizing all markers to fit the circles on the tree. If more than two players (or teams) will be playing, prepare a set of markers in a different color for each additional player. Depending on the skill you want to reinforce, you can make task cards (see page 49 or use index cards) for the game or label the game board directly. For example, to reinforce students' knowledge about snow, you might write questions on cards for use with the game. Or, to give students practice in multiplication facts, you can write a problem on each circle on the tree. If desired, prepare an answer key to make the game self-checking. To use, students place a marker on the tree for each question or problem they answer correctly. Once all of the circles are covered, students count their markers on the tree. The player with the most markers wins the game.

HOLIDAY TASK CARDS

Copy, color, and cut out the cards on page 49. There are numerous uses for these, such as for nametags, word walls, flash cards, patterning practice, or matching activities. Or, use an overhead projector to trace large images of the items onto poster board or bulletin board paper. Color, cut out and use the enlarged images to create displays or signs to post around the room.

 SNOWMAN SKILLS PUPPETS

Reinforce a variety of skills with these seasonal snowmen puppets. To begin, photocopy a supply of the snowmen patterns on pages 50–51. Color and cut out the patterns, then label each one with the particular skill you want students to practice. For example, you might write multiplication facts on the front of the snowmen and the answers on the back. Or label snowmen pairs with synonyms or antonyms. Then glue a craft stick to each snowman. To create a stand for the puppets, cover a shallow box with holiday wrapping paper. Cut slits in the box, just wide enough for inserting the craft stick handles so the puppets stand upright. To use, have students read the front of a snowman, give their response, then remove the puppet and check their answer on the back.

 ELF SKILLS WHEEL

Use the elf wheel patterns on pages 52–53 to reinforce math skills and more. To prepare, write a problem in each of the large boxes (outlined in gray). Write the answer in the small box directly opposite each problem on the left. Cut out the elf, candy cane, and wheel. Then carefully cut out the "windows" on the elf. Use one brass fastener to attach the wheel to the elf and another to attach the candy cane. To use, students turn to the wheel so that a problem appears in the right window. They solve the problem and then slide the candy cane away from the left window to check their answer.

★ MINI GREETING CARDS

Inspire creative writing with these miniature greeting cards. Distribute photocopies of page 54 and half-sheets of construction paper to students. Ask them to color and cut out the patterns of their choice and glue each one to a folded sheet of construction paper. (Have them place the straight edge of their cutout along the fold of the paper.) Students can write holiday greetings, rhymes, riddles, and so on inside their cards, or they might trace the shape over several sheets of plain paper, cut out the pages, and staple them inside the cards to create mini-books. Students can then write short stories related to the item featured on the cover of their books.

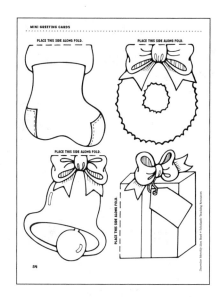

★ CORNER BOOKMARKS

These bookmarks are perfect for students to use with their favorite holiday books, or to give as gifts. Distribute photocopies of the patterns on page 55 to students. To make a bookmark, ask students to color the art, then cut out the pattern along the solid lines. Next, have them fold the wedged sections back along the dotted lines and tape the straight edges together. To use, students simply slip the bookmark over the corner of a book they are reading to mark where they left off reading or to flag a favorite page. For added flare, you might provide students with colored copies of the pattern. Or, invite them to use glitter glue, plastic gems, lace, or other craft materials to embellish their bookmarks.

★ HOLIDAY CAROLERS

Carolers bring the festive music of the season to all parts of a community. Use the cute carolers on pages 56–57 to help teach a variety of skills to your class. First, photocopy a supply of the patterns and cut out each one. You can label the carolers' songbooks with facts about Arctic animals, holiday-related vocabulary, clock stamps that show different times, and so on. Then display the carolers on a bulletin board, add a title, and attach "falling" snow to create a background. Alternately, you might use the caroler patterns as gift tags, bookmarks, name tags, or hall passes.

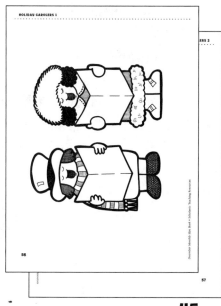

DECEMBER FUN GLASSES

Invite students to make and wear a pair of glasses that features sights of the season. First, distribute copies of the glasses patterns on page 58. Then have students color and cut out the patterns, carefully cutting the slits on the glasses frame and the earpieces. To assemble, students simply fit each earpiece into the corresponding slit on the frame. If desired, students can take their glasses home to share with family members.

 ## HOLIDAY FINGER PUPPETS

Distribute copies of the finger puppet patterns on page 59. Ask students to color and cut out the patterns. Then have them fit each puppet around their finger and secure the ends with tape. Students can use their puppets to tell about holiday events, act out stories, or dance around to songs or holiday music. Or, students might write their own stories, poems, skits, or rhymes, then use their puppets as props when presenting their written work to the class.

 ## HOLIDAY HEARTH

This holiday hearth will really help students warm up to learning! First make a photocopy of page 60 and label the stones with the skill of your choice, such as sight words, math facts, or shapes. If desired, color and cut out the hearth, laminate for durability, and place it in a learning center. Then have student pairs use the hearth to practice the targeted skills (for example, reading sight words, solving math problems, or identifying different shapes). To further reinforce skills, you might distribute photocopies of the hearth to students so they can make their own skill sheets to use for practice. In addition, you might use an overhead projector to make an enlarged copy of the hearth to use as a word wall or classroom display that features another skill students need to learn.

★ DOVE OF PEACE ORNAMENT

The December holidays often give people an opportunity to pause and reflect on the goal of peace, whether of a personal nature or for worldwide peace. Invite students to make these special dove ornaments to take home and share with their families. To begin, distribute photocopies of the dove pattern (page 61), 8-inch lengths of yarn, and tape to students. Have them do the following to make a dove:

1. Color and cut out the dove.

2. Write a message of peace on the back.

3. Fold the dove in half along the middle line. Then fold out each wing.

4. Tape a length of yarn to the top, creating a looped hanger.

★ "HOLIDAY DREAMS" STATIONERY

Students often look forward to the winter holidays with great anticipation. Set aside some time for students to share about their holiday hopes and dreams. Do they look forward to family gatherings? Giving gifts? Receiving special surprises? Enjoying favorite foods? Participating in a traditional event? After sharing, ask students to write about their expectations, hopes, and dreams for the holidays. They can write their final drafts on photocopies of page 62. Then invite students to share their written work with individual classmates or small groups.

SNOWMAN MATH

7 x 4 =

6 x 3 =

3 x 3 =

9

CUT OUT.

CUT OUT.

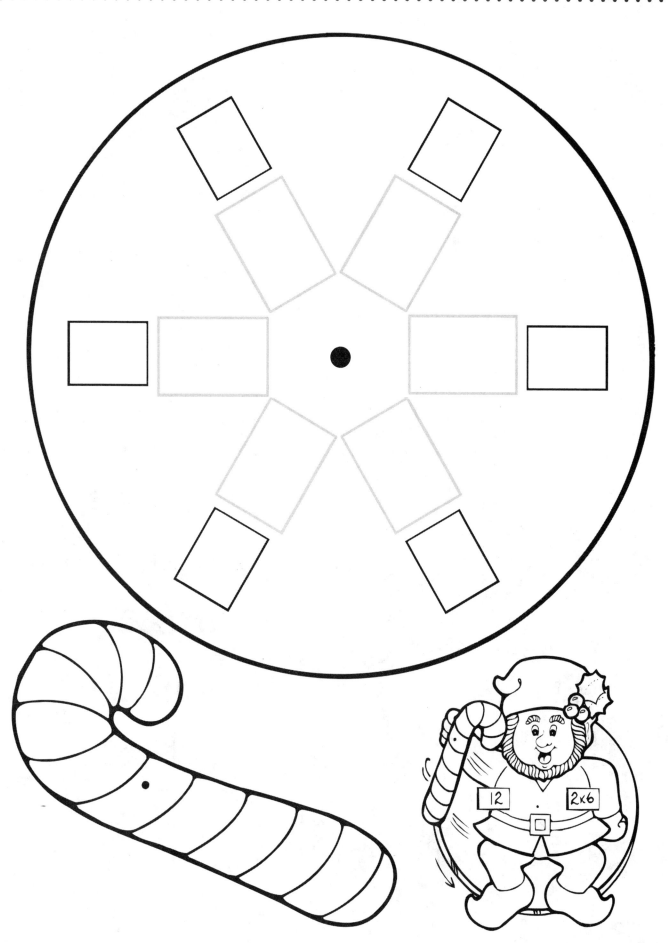

PLACE THIS SIDE ALONG FOLD.

PLACE THIS SIDE ALONG FOLD.

PLACE THIS SIDE ALONG FOLD.

PLACE THIS SIDE ALONG FOLD.

54

December Monthly Idea Book © Scholastic Teaching Resources

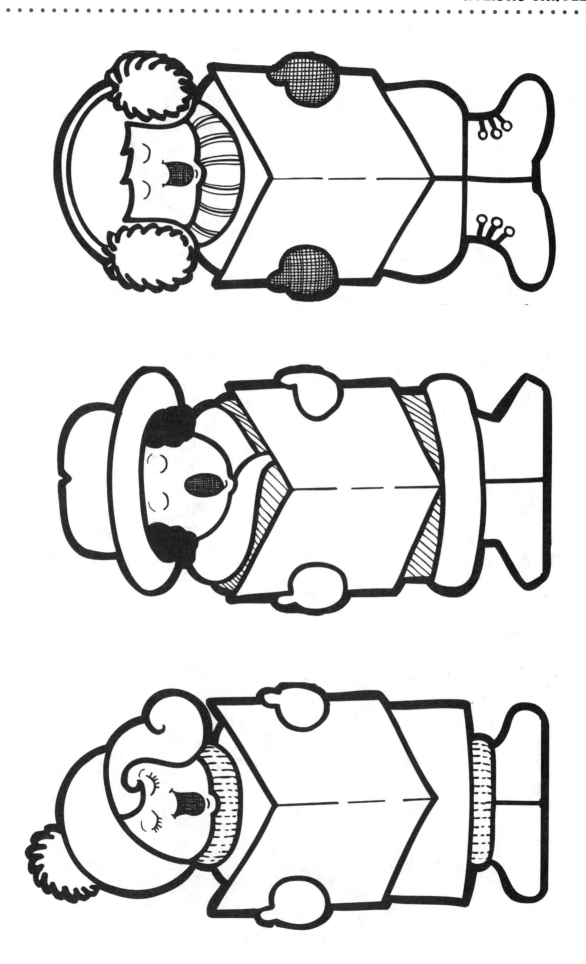

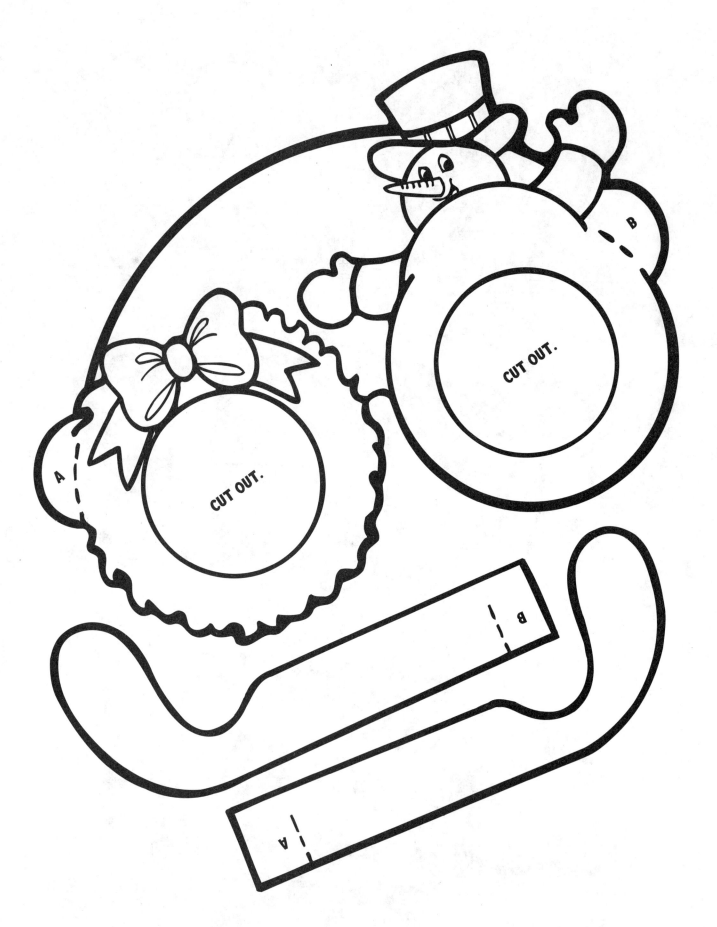

CUT OUT.

CUT OUT.

CUT OUT.

A

B

A

B

December Monthly Idea Book © Scholastic Teaching Resources

December Monthly Idea Book © Scholastic Teaching Resources

December Monthly Idea Book © Scholastic Teaching Resources

HANUKKAH: THE FESTIVAL OF LIGHTS

Hanukkah is an eight-day Jewish holiday that commemorates the Jews' successful fight for freedom over 2,000 years ago. It also celebrates a miracle that took place at that time: one day's supply of oil miraculously burned in the temple lamp for eight days. Using the Jewish calendar, which is based on the cycles of the moon, this religious festival begins the night before the twenty-fifth day of Kislev. On the western 365-day calendar, Hanukkah usually begins in late November or December.

Today, Jewish families celebrate Hanukkah—also called the Festival of Lights—by lighting candles in a menorah, a special type of candelabra. A number of other traditions that mark their religious heritage are also observed, such as telling stories, preparing latkes, playing dreidel games, and exchanging gifts.

Suggested Activities

★ MY OWN MENORAH

During Hanukkah, eight candles are placed in the menorah (one for each night of Hanukkah) plus the Shamash, or helper candle, which is positioned higher and in the center of the menorah. Explain to students that on the first night of the holiday, the Shamash is lit and then used to light one candle. On the second night, the Shamash is used to light two candles: first the new candle, then the old one. In this manner, a new candle is added and burned for each night of Hanukkah until the entire menorah glows on the eighth night.

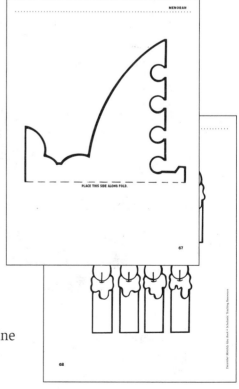

After sharing, invite students to make their own menorah. To prepare, photocopy the menorah pattern (page 67) onto several sheets of tagboard and cut out for use as templates. Then photocopy a class supply of the candle patterns (page 68) and distribute to students. (Each student should have a set of nine candles.) Provide students with the menorah templates, yellow construction paper, scissors, glue, blue and yellow crayons, and blue decorative craft items such as glitter, sequins, cellophane,

(continued)

or foil gift wrap. To make their menorah, have students do the following:

1. Fold a sheet of yellow construction paper in half.

2. Trace a menorah template onto the yellow paper, placing the straight edge along the fold. Carefully cut out the shape through both layers of paper. When unfolded, the shape will form a menorah.

3. Color and cut out the candles. Use blue for each candle and yellow for its flame. Or, instead of coloring the candles blue, decorate them with a blue craft item to add texture and sparkle.

4. Glue each candle to the menorah.

SPIN THE DREIDEL

Children often play games with dreidels, special tops labeled with Hebrew letters, as part of their Hanukkah activities. To make a dreidel for student use, photocopy the pattern on page 69 onto tagboard (use blue, if available). Cut out the pattern, then carefully cut the X on the side without a symbol. Next, fold along the dashed lines and glue the tabs in place to assemble. Finally, poke a blunt-tipped pencil through the X-shaped slit so that the pencil point rests in the point of the dreidel.

To introduce students to the significance of dreidels to Hanukkah, explain that during captivity, the Jews secretly came together to pray and study the Torah (the Jewish holy book). If an enemy came near, they hid their books and pretended to play games with their dreidels. Show students the dreidel and explain the meaning of each letter (see right). Then invite groups of three or four students to play a dreidel game, following these directions:

1. Place an empty bowl in the center of the playing area. Each player takes 10 dried beans.

2. Each player puts a bean in the bowl.

3. Players take turns spinning the dreidel. They put in or take out beans from the bowl according to the letter that lands faceup on the dreidel.

4. Whenever the bowl is emptied, each player puts one bean in to continue the game.

5. Play continues for a specified number of rounds, or until one player has won all of the beans.

Meaning:

Nun (N) means "take none"

Gimel (G) means "take all"

Heh (H) means "take half"

Shin (S) means "put one in"

ISRAEL TRADITIONAL DRESS PUPPETS

Divide the class into several groups. Explain that each group will research different aspects of life in Israel and then present their findings to the class. Assign one topic (such as food, clothing, shelter, industry, art, or transportation) to each group to research. Students can use books available in the classroom as well as library books, Internet resources, and other sources, such as videos and personal interviews for their research. Tell groups that they should look for information about life in Israel, both in the past and today to compare how the people and culture have changed with the times. Younger students will enjoy hearing you read aloud from level-appropriate books on their topic. Afterward, they can discuss the information and then write and/or draw about what they have learned.

Most groups will need a few days to complete their research for this assignment. To help students prepare their presentations, provide copies of the puppet patterns on pages 70–71 for them to cut out, color, and embellish with craft items. For example, a student might glue cloth to their puppets to represent traditional dress. They can glue wide craft sticks to their puppets to serve as handles. To extend the activity, have groups create posters to show what they've learned about their particular topic. Then invite students to use their puppets and posters to present their findings to the class.

HANUKKAH-INSPIRED WRITING

Distribute photocopies of page 72 for students to use in creative writing activities about Hanukkah-related history, traditions, symbols, activities, and so on. They might write poems, skits, short stories, songs, or imaginary tales about their topic. When finished, invite volunteers to share their written work with the class.

HANUKKAH WORD FIND

Distribute copies of the word find (page 73) to students. Explain that the word bank contains words associated with Hanukkah. Below the puzzle is an activity in which students match facts about Hanukkah. After students complete the activities, work with them to define each word in the puzzle. Provide dictionaries and other resources for students to use. Write the words and meanings on chart paper. Then encourage students to use some of the words in their Hanukkah-related writing assignments.

★ 3-D STAR OF DAVID

The blue-and-white Israeli flag features a six-pointed
star called the Star of David. This star is often used as a
symbol of Hanukkah. Invite students to make their own
Star of David ornament to add to a class display or take
home to share with their families. First, photocopy a
supply of the half-star patterns (page 74) onto tagboard
and cut out to create templates. Then provide students
with blue and white construction paper and have them do
the following to make a Star of David.

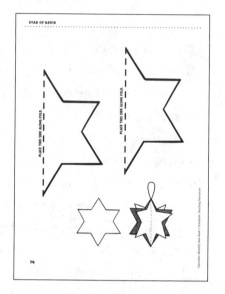

1. Fold one sheet of blue paper and two sheets of
white paper in half.

2. Trace the half-star template onto each sheet of
paper, placing the straight edge along the fold.

3. Cut out the shapes. When unfolded the shape will
be a six-pointed star.

4. Unfold the blue star. Glue only the folded edge of one of the
white stars to the center of the blue star, being careful not to
glue down the sides of the star.

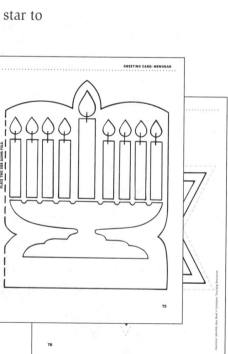

5. Turn the blue star over and repeat step 4 using the other white star.
After the glue dries, spread out the sides of the white stars.

6. Attach a length of yarn or kite string to the top of the 3-D star to
create a hanger.

★ HANUKKAH GREETING CARDS

Many families exchange gifts on each day of Hanukkah.
To commemorate this holiday tradition, set aside time
to allow students to prepare simple gifts for classmates
or family members. Provide a variety of craft items and
encourage students to use their imagination and creativity
to make unique gifts. If desired, have them create gifts that
have a Hanukkah theme or use a related symbol. Then
have them use photocopies of the greeting card patterns
on pages 75 and 76 to make cards to go with their gifts.
Or, students can use the patterns to make book covers
for their Hanukkah-related writing assignments.

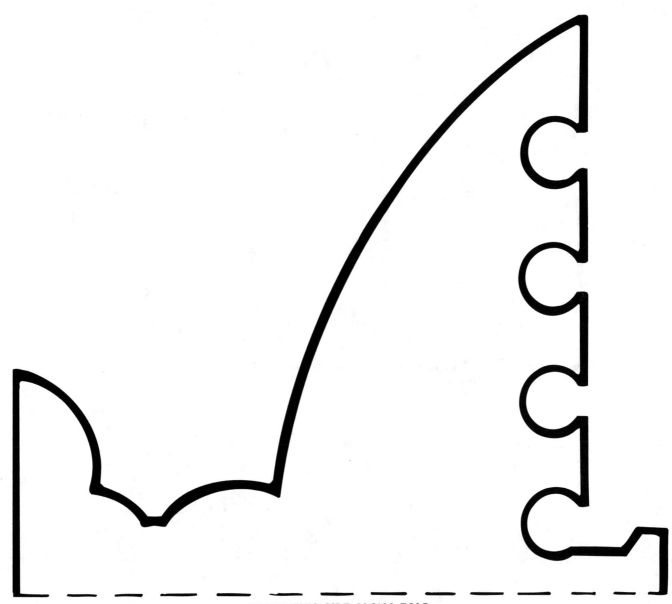

PLACE THIS SIDE ALONG FOLD.

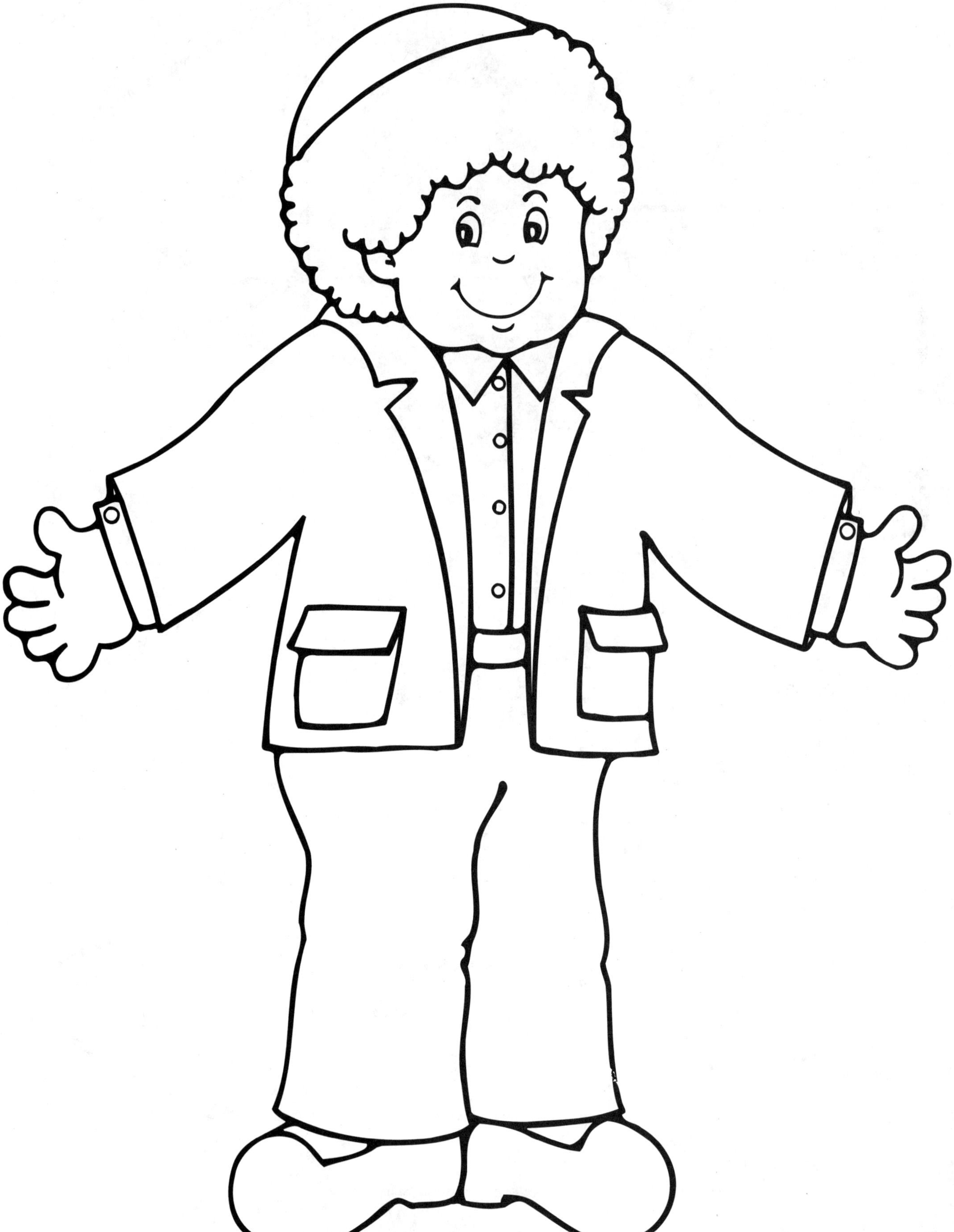

Hanukkah Word Find

Find these words in the puzzle below:

CANDLES   DREIDEL   EIGHT   FESTIVAL   GELT   HANUKKAH

JEWISH   LATKES   LIGHT   MACCABEES   MENORAH   SHAMASH

```
J W R T Y H A N U K K A H N B G F D S F G Y
E W D F T G H Y T H Y U J S E R T X Z A E T
W S F R D R E I D E L E M S E R F V X F L W
I E R D S C I G T H Y Y E D F C Y U I O T Q
S W E R T R G S E Y U I N D Q A T Y U O S M
H H A S E F H B V C S B O W X N U I O P L J
K J H G D E T W X V J K R N M D E Y U O P L
M A C C A B E E S L R T A R G L G H J U K I
A S D F R T Y H G F V B H J T E U I O P L N
A S W Q E L A T K E S F R E R S K L I G H T
X Z C V B N H Y T G F R E D S W Q M K L O P
M S H A M A S H Y B V F R E D C X S Y H K L
S E R T H J K I U Y N J P R X W Q R S G N M
W X C V G Y T R F B H U J K O P L M H Y T B
S E R F V D C T H F E S T I V A L R F G H J
```

Draw lines to match the Hanukkah facts below:

a type of top   •   • latkes

the "servant" candle   •   • Hanukkah

potato pancakes   •   • dreidel

candleholder   •   • shamash

the Festival of Lights •   • menorah

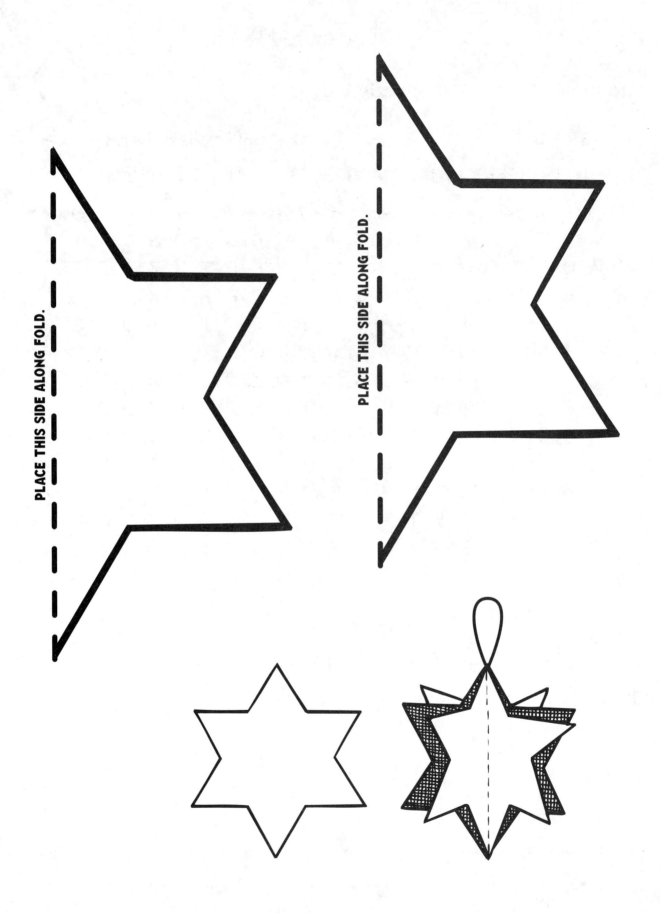

PLACE THIS SIDE ALONG FOLD.

PLACE THIS SIDE ALONG FOLD.

December Monthly Idea Book © Scholastic Teaching Resources

PLACE THIS SIDE ALONG FOLD.

PLACE THIS SIDE ALONG FOLD.

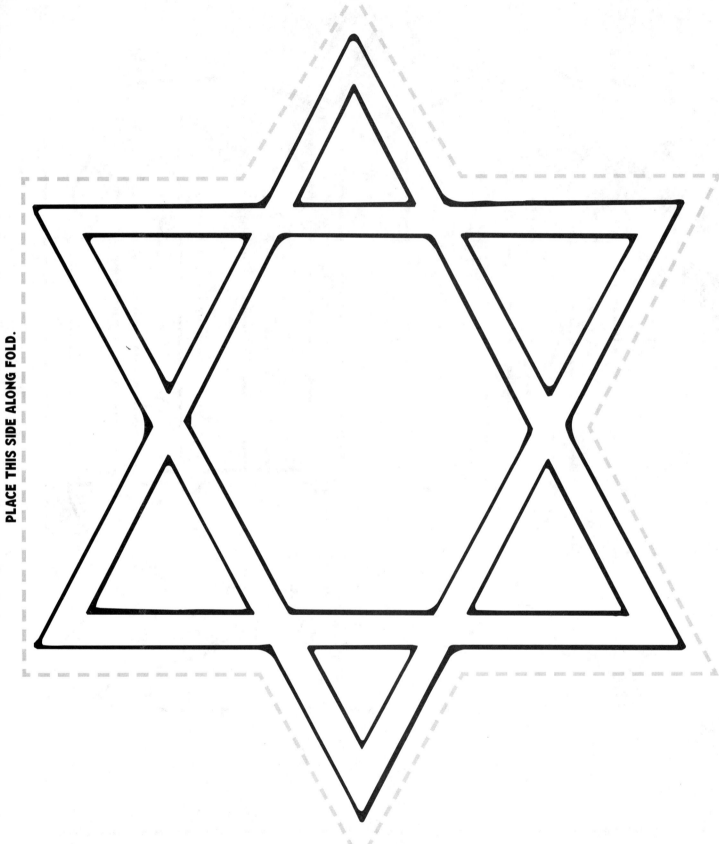

December Monthly Idea Book © Scholastic Teaching Resources

CHRISTMAS AROUND THE WORLD

Christmas is celebrated in many ways in many places across the globe. In this unit, students will explore some of the Christmas customs and traditions that other cultures follow during this worldwide holiday.

Suggested Activities

★ LANGUAGE CHART

Teach students how to say "Merry Christmas" in other languages! Simply display a photocopy of the language chart on page 89 to review how "Merry Christmas" is said in languages of interest to students. (For a resource on pronunciations, use a website that features recordings of the phrase in different languages, such as www.omniglot.com/language/phrases/christmas.htm.) To extend the activity, have students do research to discover where the different languages are spoken.

★ INTERNATIONAL CHRISTMAS TREE

According to legend, the tradition of decorating a tree for Christmas had its origins in Germany. A man named Martin Luther was so inspired by the shimmer of snow-covered evergreen branches reflecting the moonlight that he cut down a tree, brought it indoors, and decorated it with lighted candles. Over time, tree decorating became a worldwide tradition, with the type and style of decorations varying from place to place. After sharing this brief history of the Christmas tree, create an international tree for students to enjoy during the holiday season. Enlarge the tree pattern on page 90 onto poster board or bulletin board paper. Then label the ornaments with "Merry Christmas" in different languages. (Use the chart on page 89 as a reference.) Invite students to help color the tree. Finally, display the tree with the title "Merry Christmas Around the World." You might have students color their own copies of the tree (page 90) to add to the display.

COUNTRIES-AROUND-THE-WORLD WORD FIND

To familiarize students with the names of different countries around the world, have them complete the word find on page 91. After students complete the puzzle, display a large world map and help them find each country on the map. Then have them choose a country from the puzzle and complete the writing assignment at the bottom of the page.

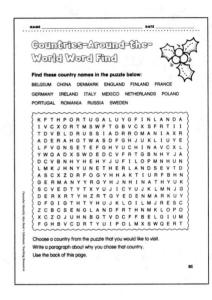

"PEACE ON EARTH" DOVE

The holiday season is a time during which people in many countries emphasize world peace. Invite students to make peace doves to express their wish for peace in different languages. First, copy the list of countries (below) and the word for "peace" in the language of each one. Review the list with students, adding any other countries and languages that are of interest to students. Then distribute a photocopy of the dove pattern (page 92) and a sheet of plain, white paper to each student. Ask students to write the word "peace"— or a short peace message—on the lower section of their dove's body. They might write the word for "peace" in the language of their choice, using the list as a reference. Next, have students cut out their dove and carefully cut a slit along the dashed line. To complete, help students fanfold their plain sheet of paper, insert it through the slit, and spread out the folds so the paper resembles a bird's outstretched wings. If desired, have students add a yarn hanger to their dove.

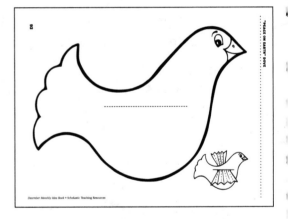

"Peace" in Different Languages			
France	Paix	Japan	Heiwa
German	Frieden	Poland	Pokój
Greece	Iríni	Russia	Mir
Ireland	Frede	Spain	Paz
Israel	Shalom	Swahili	Imani
Italy	Pace	Sweden	Fred

Christmas in the United States

Many of the Christmas customs and traditions in the United States have arisen or evolved from the cultures of other countries. Over time, though, some symbols and rituals of the holiday have become uniquely American as a result of creative story telling and commercialization of the holiday. For example, the depiction of Santa Claus in the classic story *The Night Before Christmas* helped reinvent this Christmas character into a jolly, plump elf-like figure. The story is also responsible for the image of eight flying reindeer pulling Santa's sleigh. Later, a ninth reindeer, the lovable Rudolph with a red nose that glowed, was created as part of a marketing strategy for a large department store in Chicago, Illinois.

★ LOOKING FOR SANTA

Invite students to research and write about how the American version of Santa Claus came about and evolved. They can use a variety of resources such as nonfiction books, the Internet, videos, documentaries, and personal interviews to gather their information. Have students write the final draft of their findings on photocopies of the stationery on page 93. Once they complete their reports, invite students to share them with the class. If desired, collect the reports and use a photocopy of page 94 to make a cover for them. Add a title and your class name to the cover, invite a volunteer to color it, then place the book in your class library.

★ SANTA ORNAMENT

Students can use this adorable Santa ornament as a table centerpiece, gift, or storytelling prop. Or, you might add the ornaments to your class holiday tree. To make the ornaments, have students color and cut out a photocopy of the pattern on page 95. Then instruct them to fold the ornament along the dashed lines to form a pyramid-like shape and secure with tape. If desired, have students glue stretched cotton balls to Santa's beard. Finally, help them add a yarn hanger to the top of their ornament.

★ THE NIGHT BEFORE CHRISTMAS

Read aloud Clement C. Moore's *The Night Before Christmas* and discuss the Christmas symbols, rituals, and activities in the story. Point out that flying reindeer are often associated with Christmas, but real reindeer can't fly. Then have students research reindeer and write about their findings. To make a page framer for their written work, ask students to color and cut out photocopies of the reindeer patterns on page 96. Have them glue their reindeer's head and tail to opposite ends of a brown sheet of construction paper. Then, for legs, help students fanfold four 12-inch strips of brown paper and attach them to the bottom of their reindeer body, as shown. Finally, have students attach their pages to the page framer and display on a bulletin board.

★ STAND-UP STORY PROPS

Invite students to make stand-up reindeer and sleighs to use in Christmas-related role-playing and storytelling. For the reindeer, have students color and cut out tagboard photocopies of the pattern on page 97. Then have them fold their cutout on the dashed line to create a stand-up reindeer. If desired, students can glue sand to the antlers to add texture.

To make the sleigh, give each student two tagboard photocopies of the pattern on page 98 and four 4-inch lengths of drinking straws. Have students color and cut out their sleighs and then punch four holes in each cutout where indicated. To assemble, help students insert their four straws into the holes to connect the two sleigh cutouts, as shown.

STOCKING STUFFERS

On Christmas morning, many children wake up to stockings stuffed with goodies and gifts. What do students hope to find in their Christmas stockings? After sharing, distribute copies of the stationery on page 99. Have students write about their Christmas hopes and wishes. Students can also use the stationery for other Christmas-related creative writing assignments, such as poems, songs, acrostics, or imaginary stories about Christmas celebrations, characters, and activities.

HOLIDAY WORD FIND

Distribute copies of the word find on page 100. Explain to students that the word bank on the page contains words associated with Christmas in the United States. Review the words, then ask students to find and circle each one in the puzzle. After students complete the puzzle, have them unscramble the names of Santa's reindeer at the bottom of the page.

Christmas in Mexico

In Mexico, Las Posadas—a nine-day celebration that commemorates the biblical story of Mary and Joseph's trip to Bethlehem and their search for lodging—is observed from December 16–24. Each night, in a reenactment of the couple's journey, two children carrying small figures of the Holy Family lead a procession of *pereginos* (pilgrims) from house to house looking for *posada*, or shelter. They are turned away each time, until the last night, Christmas Eve. On that night, the door of the last house is open to the peregrinos. There, they enter and the lead children place the figures of the Mary and Joseph in a manger scene. After a time of prayer and worship, Las Posadas ends with fun and festivities, including breaking a piñata filled with candy, fruit, and gifts.

★ LAS POSADAS PICTURE PROPS

Prepare a set of picture props for students to use in sharing information and stories related to Las Posadas. Color, cut out, and laminate tagboard photocopies of the pictures on pages 101–103. Then attach hook-and-loop fasteners to the back of the images for use with a flannelboard. Or, affix adhesive magnet strips for use with a magnet board. If desired, have students do research to learn more about Las Posadas. Invite them to use the picture props to share what they have learned.

★ LAS POSADAS CANDLE

Candles play an important role in a Las Posadas procession. *Farolitos*, small bags with candles in them, light up the path along which the peregrinos travel. Invite students to make a candle that they can carry when reenacting a Las Posadas procession. Or, they can place their candle in a paper bag to give as a surprise gift to someone special. Provide each student with a 4-inch cardboard tube, plastic yogurt lid, colorful tissue paper, yellow and green construction paper, red sequins, and tape. Then have them do the following the make their candle:

1. Cover the tube with tissue paper. Cover one of the ends with tissue paper as well.

2. Tape the tube (candle) to the plastic lid, as shown.

3. Cut out a yellow construction-paper flame, as shown. Fold the bottom tab and tape the flame to the top of the candle.

4. Cut out green leaves to tape around the base of the candle. (Use rolled pieces of tape.) Add red sequins to represent holly berries.

★ MINIATURE PIÑATA ORNAMENT

Invite students to make miniature piñata ornaments to give as gifts or to use when sharing what they know about Las Posadas. You might add the ornaments to your class holiday tree to give it an international flavor. To prepare, give each student an egg-carton eggcup and an 8-inch length of yarn. Also, provide fabric or glitter pens, shredded strips of paper, treats small enough to fit inside an eggcup, and tape. Then have students do the following to make a piñata:

1. Use fabric or glitter pens to decorate the eggcup.

2. Knot one end of the yarn. Poke the other end through the inside bottom of the eggcup and pull the yarn out as far as it will go. (The knot will hold the other end in place.)

3. Glue strips of shredded paper around the edge of the eggcup to create a fringe.

4. Use rolled tape to fasten a small treat to the inside of the eggcup.

★ "FELIZ NAVIDAD!" BULLETIN BOARD

In Mexico, people say *Feliz Navidad* to wish others a merry Christmas. Invite students to do research to learn more about how Christmas is celebrated in Mexico. Have them write their findings on copies of the stationery on page 104. Then create a festive-looking bulletin board on which to display students' work. First, on poster board cut out a large animal outline, such as a bird. Cover the shape with strips of colored, fringed tissue paper and add facial features and other characteristics so that it resembles a piñata. Attach the "piñata" to a bulletin board and add yarn so that it appears to be hanging from the top of the board. Top the display with the title "Feliz Navidad!" Finally, post students' reports around the piñata.

Christmas in Italy

In Italy, Christmas is a time of family gatherings, worship, and celebration. In some parts of the country, musicians dressed in traditional costumes travel from town to town playing their bagpipes and flutes in town squares and around churches. Often, a nativity scene, or *presipio*, is displayed in churches and many homes. During the days leading up to Christmas, families gather around the presipio and pray. They fast for 24 hours beginning at sunset on December 23. On Christmas Eve, many attend worship services at their churches. At home, children take turns telling the wonderful story of the birth of the holy *bambino*. On Christmas Day, families enjoy a feast of traditional foods, including pastas such as spaghetti and lasagna.

★ LA BEFANA PAPER-BAG PUPPET

Although *Babbo Natale* (or Santa Claus) delivers some gifts on Christmas Day, the main day of gift giving occurs on the twelfth day of Christmas (January 6th, the Feast of Ephiphany). According to legend, a kind witch named *La Befana* leaves gifts for children at this time. Work with students to learn about the story of Le Befana. Then distribute small paper bags and photocopies of the patterns on page 105. Have students color and cut out the patterns, then glue La Befana's head to the bottom flap of the bag and her mouth to the front below the flap. Students can use craft items, such as torn pieces of tissue paper, glitter glue, or ribbon, to add embellishments to their puppets.

★ LA BEFANA ORNAMENT

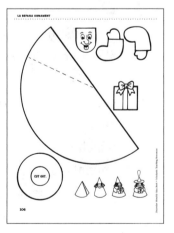

Students can use this La Befana ornament to tell her story to family members. Or, add the ornaments to your class holiday tree to give it an international flavor. Distribute photocopies of page 106 to students. (You might copy the semicircle on colorful sheets of paper.) Then provide tape, glue, and yarn. Have students do the following to make their ornament:

1. Color and cut out the patterns. Carefully cut out the center of the circle to form a ring—this is the brim of La Befana's hat.

2. Form the semicircle into a cone and secure with tape.

3. Glue the face to the cone about 1½ inches below the point. Add short lengths of yarn for hair, as shown on page 106. Then glue on the arms and gift.

4. Place the hat brim (paper ring) over the top of the cone. Slide it down until it fits snugly above La Befana's face. (Secure with tape, if needed.)

5. Add a yarn hanger to the top of the hat.

★ ITALY TRADITIONAL DRESS PUPPETS

Divide the class into several groups and explain that students will research different aspects of life in Italy. Assign one topic (such as food, clothing, shelter, industry, art, or transportation) to each group. Then have students use classroom and library books, Internet resources, and other sources, such as videos and documentaries, to find information about life in Italy, both in the past and today to compare how the people and culture have changed with the times. Younger students will enjoy hearing you read aloud from level-appropriate books on their topic. Afterward, they can discuss the information and write and/or draw about what they have learned.

To help students prepare their presentations, invite them to cut out and color photocopies of the puppet patterns on pages 107–108. If desired, they can embellish their puppets with craft items, such as cloth and ribbons, to represent traditional dress. Then instruct students to glue craft-stick handles to their puppets. To extend the activity, have groups create posters to show what they've learned about their particular topic. Finally, invite students to use their puppets and posters to present their findings to the class.

★ AN ITALIAN CHRISTMAS

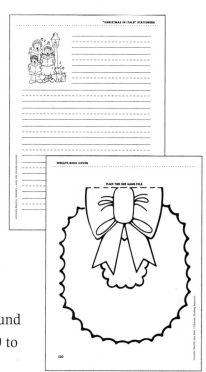

Invite students to write about Christmas in Italy. Encourage them to consider a variety of ways to convey their thoughts and knowledge. For instance, students might write a poem about La Befana, compose song lyrics that depict a traditional Christmas celebration, or write an imaginative story from a traveling musician's perspective to describe the holiday sights and sounds. Distribute photocopies of the stationery on page 109 for students to use for their final drafts.

★ WREATH BOOK COVER

Tell students that some believe the tradition of displaying wreaths at Christmas began in Italy. The ancient Romans hung wreaths as a symbol of victory. Today, wreaths are used in holiday celebrations around the world. After sharing, invite students to use the pattern on page 110 to make covers for their reports or other writing about Christmas in Italy.

Christmas in Holland / The Netherlands

In the Netherlands, holiday gifts for younger children are given on December 6—Sinterklaas Day. This date marks the name day of Saint Nicolas, the patron saint of children and sailors. According to tradition, "Sinterklaas" (Santa Clause) arrives around mid-November on a large steamboat from his home in Spain. He brings his white horse and dozens of helpers along with him. In the weeks before Sinterklaas Day, children are on their best behavior as they and their families prepare for the holidays. On Sinterklaas Eve, children leave a shoe by the fireplace or door in anticipation of Sinterklaas' arrival. Often they put carrot sticks or hay in their shoe as a treat for Sinterklaas' horse. Then, on December 6, they awaken to find the horse treats replaced with candy or small presents (if they have been "good" children). Often, they discover additional gifts left by Sinterklaas, or a note telling them where they can find their gifts.

 ## WOODEN SHOE WISHES

Invite students to make wooden shoes to write their holiday gift wishes on. (Explain that wooden shoes, or clogs, are traditional footwear in the Dutch culture.) Distribute photocopies of the patterns on page 111. Ask students to write their name on the shoe and color and cut out all of the patterns. Then have them glue the carrot and hay "in" the shoe. To complete, instruct students to write about, draw, or glue pictures (from catalogs or magazines) of their gift wishes on the back of their shoe.

 ## WINDMILL ORNAMENT

 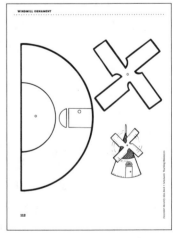

Windmills are often associated with Holland and are still used today for land drainage and many other purposes. Invite students to make a windmill ornament to take home. Or, add the windmill ornaments to your class holiday tree to give it an international flavor. To begin, distribute tagboard photocopies of the patterns on page 112. Ask students to color and cut out each piece. Then have them form the semicircle into a cone and secure with tape—this will be the windmill base. Next, help students use a brass fastener to attach the blades where indicated. Finally, have students attach a yarn hanger to the top of their windmill ornament.

December Monthly Idea Book © Scholastic Teaching Resources

★ HOLLAND TRADITIONAL DRESS PUPPETS

Pair up students to write reports about topics related to life in Holland (such as food, clothing, shelter, industry, art, or transportation). Assign a topic to each pair and have students research library books, the Internet, and other sources to learn about their topic. Encourage them to write a report about their findings, using photocopies of the stationery on page 115 for their final draft. Then have students make one or both of the puppets (pages 113–114) to use as props for their presentations. After they color and cut out their puppets, students can embellish them with craft items, such as scraps of cloth, glitter, lace, and ribbon, to represent the traditional dress of Holland. To complete, have students glue a craft-stick handle to their puppets. Finally, invite students to use their puppets to present their reports.

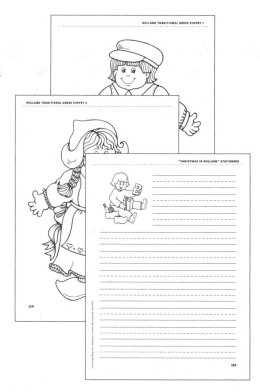

★ WINDMILL BOOKLET

Sinterklaas Day is a festive time filled with celebrations and merriment. Christmas Day, however, is a much quieter occasion on which families gather for church services and meals. Families may also exchange a few gifts on Christmas Day, but most gifts have already been given on Sinterklaas Day. Ask students to do research about the Christmas season in Holland to learn more. Then have them write short stories, poems, songs, skits, or imaginary tales about the holiday. Or, they might compare a Holland Christmas to their own family celebrations. When finished, invite students to make a windmill book cover to use with their written work. Photocopy a class supply of page 116 onto plain paper and page 117 onto tagboard. Then distribute a copy of each pattern, a large sheet of construction paper, and a paper fastener to each student. To make their book covers, have students do the following:

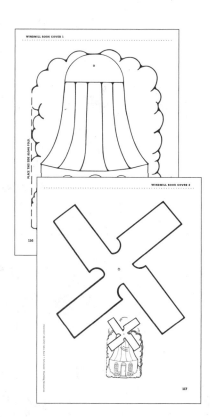

1. Color and cut out the front cover reproducibles.

2. Fold the sheet of construction paper in half. Glue on the cover (the windmill base), placing the straight edge along the fold.

3. Cut out the windmill blades.

4. Use the paper fastener to attach the blades to just the front cover.

5. Staple the written pages inside the cover.

Christmas in Sweden

The Christmas season in Sweden begins with Saint Lucia Day on December 13, one of the shortest days of the year. During this celebration, the eldest daughter (or mother) in a family dons a white gown, wears an evergreen wreath with lighted candles on her head, and serves sweet cakes and coffee to her family members in their beds.

★ SAINT LUCIA HEAD WREATH

Have students use a variety of sources to learn about Saint Lucia Day and then make Saint Lucia head wreaths. First, help students fit a strip of green construction paper around their head to make a headband. Then give each student two photocopies of page 118. Have students color and cut out the patterns and glue them to their headband, as shown on page 118. Students might also color and cut out a photocopy of the picture prop on page 119. They can wear their wreath and use the picture prop to share what they know about Saint Lucia Day.

★ SWEDEN TRADITIONAL DRESS PUPPET

Divide the class into several groups and have each group research different aspects of Swedish life. (Assign topics such as food, clothing, shelter, industry, art, or transportation.) Students can use library books, Internet resources, and other sources for their research. Have the groups look for information about life in Sweden, both in the past and today to compare how the people and culture have changed with the times. After groups complete their research, provide copies of the puppet pattern on page 120 for students to cut out, color, and embellish with craft items. (Students might also make their own traditional-dress female puppet, or use the picture prop on page 119.) To complete, have them glue craft-stick handles to their puppet. Finally, invite students to use their puppet to present their research to the class.

★ SAINT LUCIA DAY STATIONERY

Distribute photocopies of page 121 for students to use in creative writing projects about Saint Lucia Day or Christmas-related activities in Sweden. They might write poems, skits, short stories, songs, or imaginary tales about their topic.

MERRY CHRISTMAS AROUND THE WORLD

Chinese	**Shèng Dàn Kuài Lè**
Danish	**Glaedelig Jul**
Dutch	**Vrolijk Kerstfeest**
English	**Merry Christmas**
Finnish	**Hyvää Joulua**
French	**Joyeux Noël**
German	**Fröhliche Weihnachten**
Greek	**Kala Christouyenna**
Irish	**Nollaig Shona Dhuit**
Italian	**Buon Natale**
Japanese	**Kurisumasu Omedeto**
Portuguese	**Feliz Natal**
Russian	**S Rozhdestvom Khristovym**
Spanish	**Feliz Navidad**
Swahili	**Heri La Krismasi**
Swedish	**God Jul**

Countries-Around-the-World Word Find

Find these country names in the puzzle below:

BELGIUM   CHINA   DENMARK   ENGLAND   FINLAND   FRANCE

GERMANY   IRELAND   ITALY   MEXICO   NETHERLANDS   POLAND

PORTUGAL   ROMANIA   RUSSIA   SWEDEN

```
K F T H P O R T U G A L U Y G F I N L A N D A
I V C X O R T M S W F T G B V C X S F R T I I
T D V B L D R U S S I A D R R O M A N I A X R
A D E R A H G T W A S D F G H J U K L I U Y E
L F V G N S E T E F G H Y U C H I N A V C X L
Y W Q A D X S W D E D C V F R T G B N H Y J A
D C V B N H Y H E H Y J U F I L O P M N H U N
L M K J H N Y U N E T H E R L A N D S E V T D
A S C X Z D R F O G Y H H A K T I U R F B H N
G E R M A N Y Y R G Y H J N H I N A T H Y U K
S C V E D T Y T X Y U J I C Y U J K L M N J G
D E R X R T Y H Z R T G Y E D E N M A R K U Y
D F G I G T H T Y H U J K L O I L M J R E S C
Z C B C S E N G L A N D F R T H N M K L O P O
X C Z O J U H N B G T V D C F F B E L G I U M
F G H B V C D R T Y U I P O L M X S W Q E R T
```

Choose a country from the puzzle that you would like to visit.

Write a paragraph about why you chose that country.

Use the back of this page.

December Monthly Idea Book © Scholastic Teaching Resources

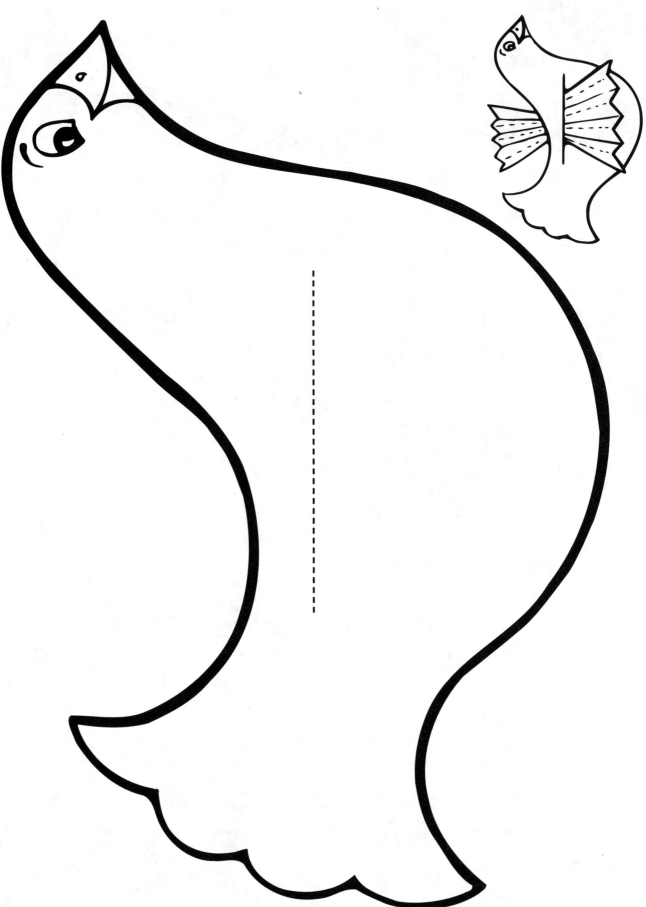

PLACE THIS SIDE ALONG FOLD.

December Monthly Idea Book © Scholastic Teaching Resources

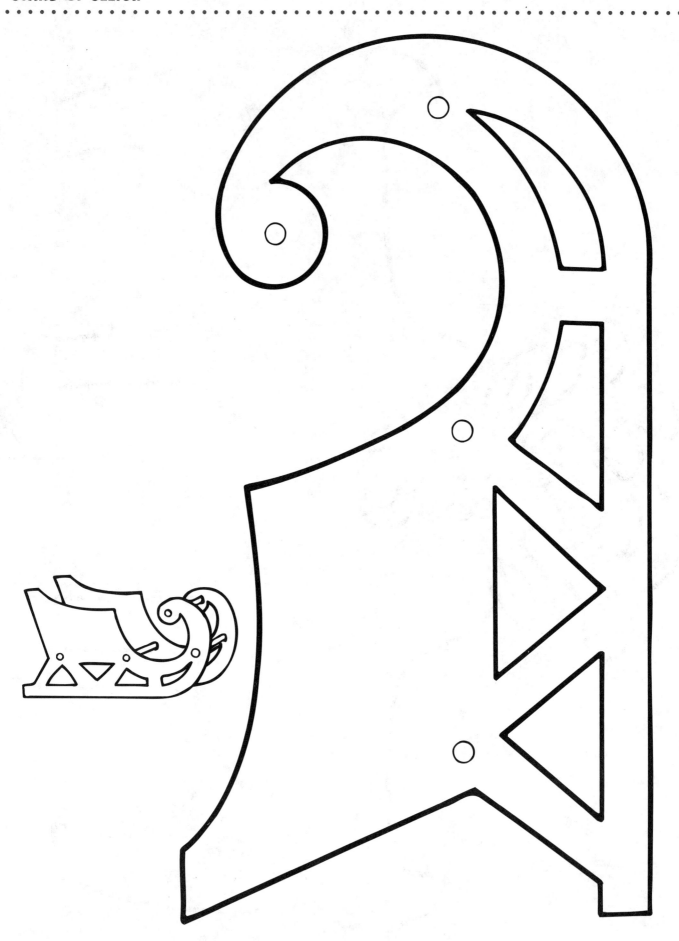

Holiday Word Find

Find these words in the puzzle below:

BELLS   BOWS   GARLAND   ICICLES   LIGHTS

ORNAMENTS   REINDEER   SANTA   STAR   TINSEL

```
W C V G H J B O W S S D F G Y S T A R F
S D R T G F H R Y N J H U I K D E R T I
G G T Y H J U N R E W Q R T Y U I K L C
A D E R T H S A N T A C P N E S K L J I
R F T Y J G H M N B Y N A L R U D R T C
L F G T H Y N E J K R E W X Z A P G W L
A D E R T Y H N D F B C F R T Y H J H E
N F T F T G H T I N S E L B H J U I L S
D F G T H Y U S K I L O J E F T G H U J
R E I N D E E R S T Y H N L G Y U I P R
B G H U Y T F G H J U I K L G V B N M K
S E R T H J U I L I G H T S E D C V B N
```

Unscramble the names of Santa's reindeer.
Use the names in the box to help you.

P D I U C   __ __ __ __ __

X I N V E   __ __ __ __ __

Z N E T I L B   __ __ __ __ __ __ __

H S R E A D   __ __ __ __ __ __

M O T E C   __ __ __ __ __

C A N D R E   __ __ __ __ __ __

D U L O H P R   __ __ __ __ __ __ __

C R N E A R P   __ __ __ __ __ __ __

D D N O R E   __ __ __ __ __ __

Blitzen	Donder
Comet	Prancer
Cupid	Rudolph
Dancer	Vixen
Dasher	

December Monthly Idea Book © Scholastic Teaching Resources

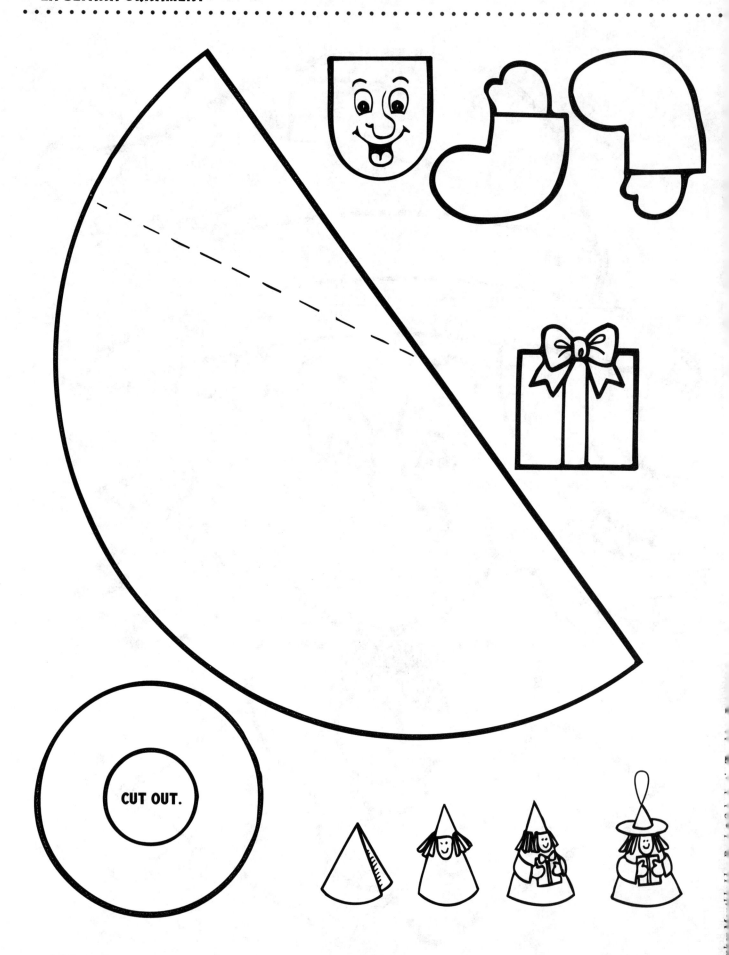

CUT OUT.

PLACE THIS SIDE ALONG FOLD.

December Monthly Idea Book © Scholastic Teaching Resources

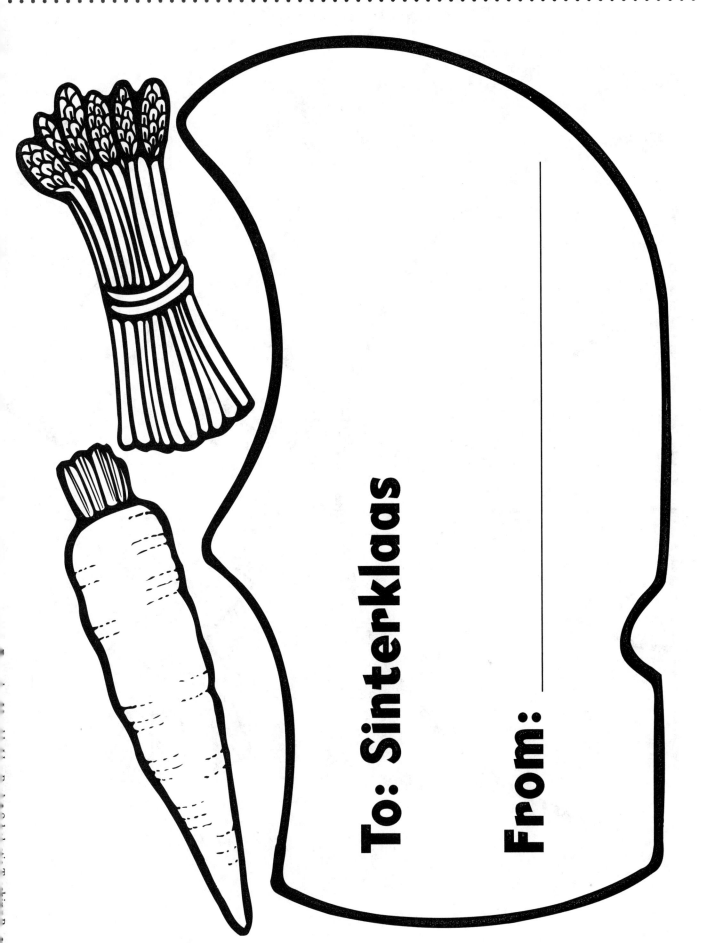

To: Sinterklaas

From: _____

December Monthly Idea Book © Scholastic Teaching Resources

PLACE THIS SIDE ALONG FOLD.

December Monthly Idea Book © Scholastic Teaching Resources

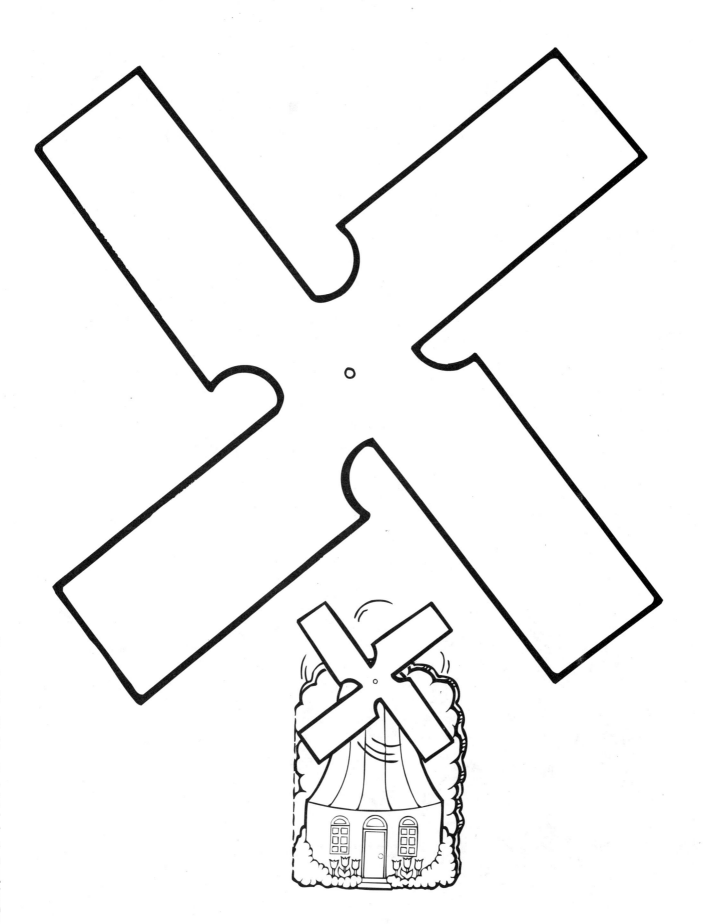

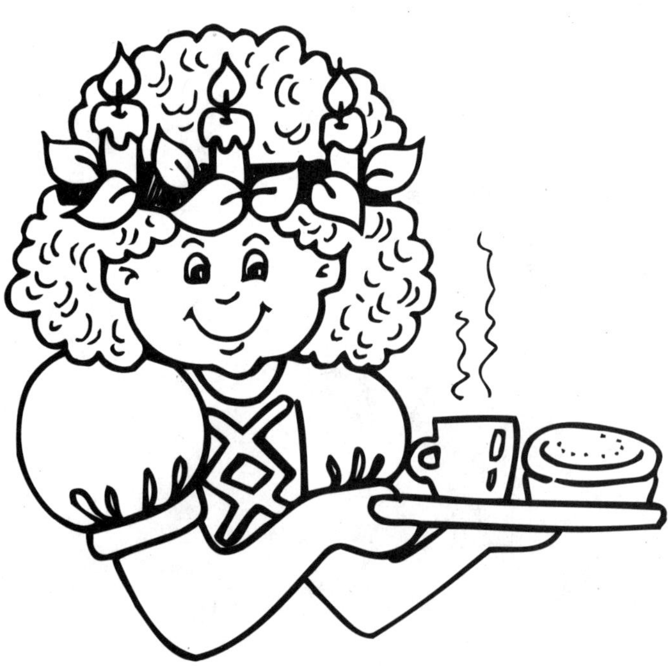

KWANZAA: A CULTURAL CELEBRATION

The seven-day Kwanzaa holiday is celebrated from December 26 to January 1. Created by Dr. Maulana Karenga in 1966, this modern African American celebration was developed to help promote and preserve traditional African values and customs. From its name—*Kwanzaa*, which is Swahili for "first fruits"—to its focus on seven important principles and the use of seven representative symbols, this weeklong holiday encourages Americans of African descent to come together to honor their heritage, evaluate their lives, make commitments to one another and their community, express gratitude for the goodness of life, and make plans for the future.

Suggested Activities

 ## PRINCIPLES OF KWANZAA BANNER

The Kwanzaa celebration focuses on seven important principles with emphasis on a different principle each day. To share the principles with students, distribute photocopies of page 127. Review and discuss each principle. Then have students cut out their banner, glue it to a large sheet of white construction paper, and create a border using the colors of Kwanzaa: black, red, and green. To create a hanger, help students punch a hole near each top corner of their banner and tie a length of yarn to the holes. Encourage students to take the banners home to share with their families.

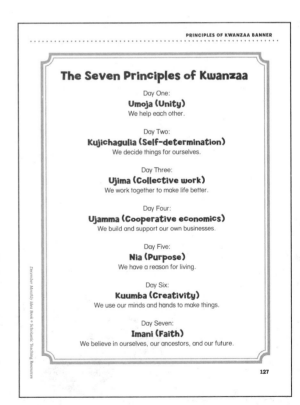

The Seven Principles of Kwanzaa

Day One:
Umoja (Unity)
We help each other.

Day Two:
Kujichagulia (Self-determination)
We decide things for ourselves.

Day Three:
Ujima (Collective work)
We work together to make life better.

Day Four:
Ujamma (Cooperative economics)
We build and support our own businesses.

Day Five:
Nia (Purpose)
We have a reason for living.

Day Six:
Kuumba (Creativity)
We use our minds and hands to make things.

Day Seven:
Imani (Faith)
We believe in ourselves, our ancestors, and our future.

December Monthly Idea Book • Scholastic Teaching Resources

127

122

SYMBOLS OF KWANZAA

During a Kwanzaa celebration, seven symbols are used, each representing a different idea. Name and explain the symbols to students. Discuss the meaning of the symbols and invite students to share about how some of these symbols might be similar to symbols used in other holidays they are familiar with (such as Hanukkah and Christmas).

kinara: a candleholder that holds seven candles—one for each day of Kwanzaa

mishumma: the seven candles (one black, three red, and three green), each representing a principle of Kwanzaa

mkeka: a woven mat that symbolizes the foundation of tradition and history

muhindi: harvested corn that symbolizes hope for the future and the value of children to the family unit (Each child is represented by one ear of corn.)

mazao: fruits and vegetables that represent the harvest and the importance of working together

zawadi: simple gifts (often hand-crafted) that symbolize the commitment between parents and children

kibombe cha umoja: a unity cup used to toast the family's ancestors

 ## KINARA CANDLES

Distribute photocopies of the kinara (page 128) to students. Explain that a kinara is a special candleholder used during the Kwanzaa celebration. The seven candles represent the seven principles of Kwanzaa, and one candle is lit each day, following a specific color order. Three red candles sit in the left side of the kinara, three green in the right side, and a single black candle sits in the middle. When lighting the candles, the black candle is lit first, then the others are lit in the order shown on students' kinaras.

After sharing, invite students to color their kinara and the candles, checking that they color the seven candles according to their placement in the kinara (from left to right: red, red, red, black, green, green, green). Finally, have students "light" the candles in order by coloring one candle flame at a time. They can use the numbers on the candles to help them follow the correct order. When finished, chorally count the candles with students, having them point to each candle in the order it should be lit. For additional fun, teach students how to count the candles in Swahili (see right).

Count in Swahili!

1—moja

2—mbili

3—tatu

4—nne

5—tano

6—sita

7—saba

MAKE AN MKEKA

The mkeka (em-KAY-kah) in a Kwanzaa celebration represents the history and foundation of the African American people. This special mat is usually placed on a table, and the other Kwanzaa symbols are set on it. Invite students to make their own mkeka with this simple idea. Set out shallow trays of red and green paint and several wooden cubes beside each tray. Then distribute sheets of black construction paper to students. Have them use the cubes and paint to stamp a red and green weave pattern onto their black paper. After the mats dry, use them as a background for a classroom Kwanzaa display, or invite students to use them in their Kwanzaa role-playing or dramatizations.

MUHINDI BOOK COVER

One ear of corn, or muhindi, represents each child in a family or household. Distribute photocopies of page 129, then instruct students to do the following to create books about themselves:

1. Color and cut out the corn pattern.

2. Glue the cutout to a sheet of construction paper to make a cover for your book. Write your name on the cover.

3. On several sheets of plain paper, write information about yourself. *What makes you special? What unique skills do you have? What are some of your favorites, such as foods, sports, books, and movies?* Add drawings to your pages, if desired.

4. Staple your pages to your cover.

Invite students to share their completed books with the class. Then collect the books and place them in your class library for others to enjoy. Or, display each student's book with his or her mkeka (see above).

★ MARVELOUS MAZAO

Students can make this bowl full of harvest foods to represent the Kwanzaa symbol of mazao. Distribute photocopies of the patterns on page 130 to students, along with large sheets of brown construction paper. Ask students to color and cut out the fruits and vegetables. Then help them trim the bottom corners of their brown paper to create a large bowl. Next, have students cut a slit across the middle of their bowl, insert each of their food cutouts partially into the slit, then glue in place. If desired, display students' mazao with their mkekas and/or muhindi books (see page 124).

★ A SPECIAL UNITY CUP

On each night of the Kwanzaa celebration, family members take a drink from the unity cup to symbolize they are one people. Invite students to create a design for a unity cup. Distribute photocopies of the cup on page 131 along with red, green, and black crayons. Encourage students to use the Kwanzaa colors to draw a simple design or pattern on their cup. Once they have completed their design, provide students with clear plastic cups and red, green, and black fabric paints or permanent markers. Instruct them to try to duplicate their unity cup pattern onto a plastic cup. Afterward, students can take their drawing and actual unity cup home to share with their family.

★ KWANZAA PICTURE PROPS

Create a set of picture props for students to use when sharing what they have learned about Kwanzaa. First, photocopy, color, and cut out the patterns on page 132. (You might also use pages 128, 130, and 131.) Laminate the pieces, then attach a hook-and-loop fastener to the back of each image for use with a flannelboard. Or, affix adhesive magnet strips to the pieces for use with a magnet board. Then invite individuals, pairs, or small groups to use the props to describe a Kwanzaa celebration or tell stories related to Kwanzaa.

★ DRAMATIC DASHIKIS

Kwanzaa celebrants often wear brightly colored clothing that reflects the brilliant designs of African art and life. Invite students to make a dashiki—an African shirt worn by both males and females—that they can wear to present their projects (see below) or during classroom Kwanzaa activities. Provide students with large brown paper bags, scissors, and drawing utensils, such as markers, crayons, and glitter pens. Then have them do the following:

1. Cut an opening up the back panel of a paper bag. Then cut the neck and arms from the bag, as shown. Leave the flaps attached to serve as sleeves, or cut them off to make a sleeveless dashiki.

2. Decorate the dashiki with colorful designs or patterns.

3. To put on, simply slide both arms into the armholes through the back opening of the dashiki.

★ AFRICA TRADITIONAL DRESS PUPPETS

Divide the class into several groups and explain that students will research different aspects of life in Africa. Assign one topic (such as food, clothing, shelter, industry, art, or transportation) to each group. Then have students use classroom and library books, Internet resources, and other sources, such as videos and personal interviews, to find information about life in Africa, both in the past and today to compare how the people and culture have changed with the times.

To help students prepare their presentations, invite them to cut out and color photocopies of the puppet patterns on pages 133–134. If desired, they can embellish their puppets with craft items, such as cloth or ribbon, to represent traditional dress. Then instruct students to glue craft-stick handles to their puppets. To extend the activity, have groups create posters to show what they've learned about their particular topic. Finally, invite students to use their puppets and posters to present their findings to the class.

★ KWANZAA-INSPIRED WRITING

Distribute photocopies of page 135 for students to use in creative writing projects about Kwanzaa-related history, traditions, symbols, activities, and so on. They might write poems, skits, short stories, songs, or imaginary tales about their topic.

The Seven Principles of Kwanzaa

Day One:
Umoja (Unity)
We help each other.

Day Two:
Kujichagulia (Self-determination)
We decide things for ourselves.

Day Three:
Ujima (Collective work)
We work together to make life better.

Day Four:
Ujamma (Cooperative economics)
We build and support our own businesses.

Day Five:
Nia (Purpose)
We have a reason for living.

Day Six:
Kuumba (Creativity)
We use our minds and hands to make things.

Day Seven:
Imani (Faith)
We believe in ourselves, our ancestors, and our future.

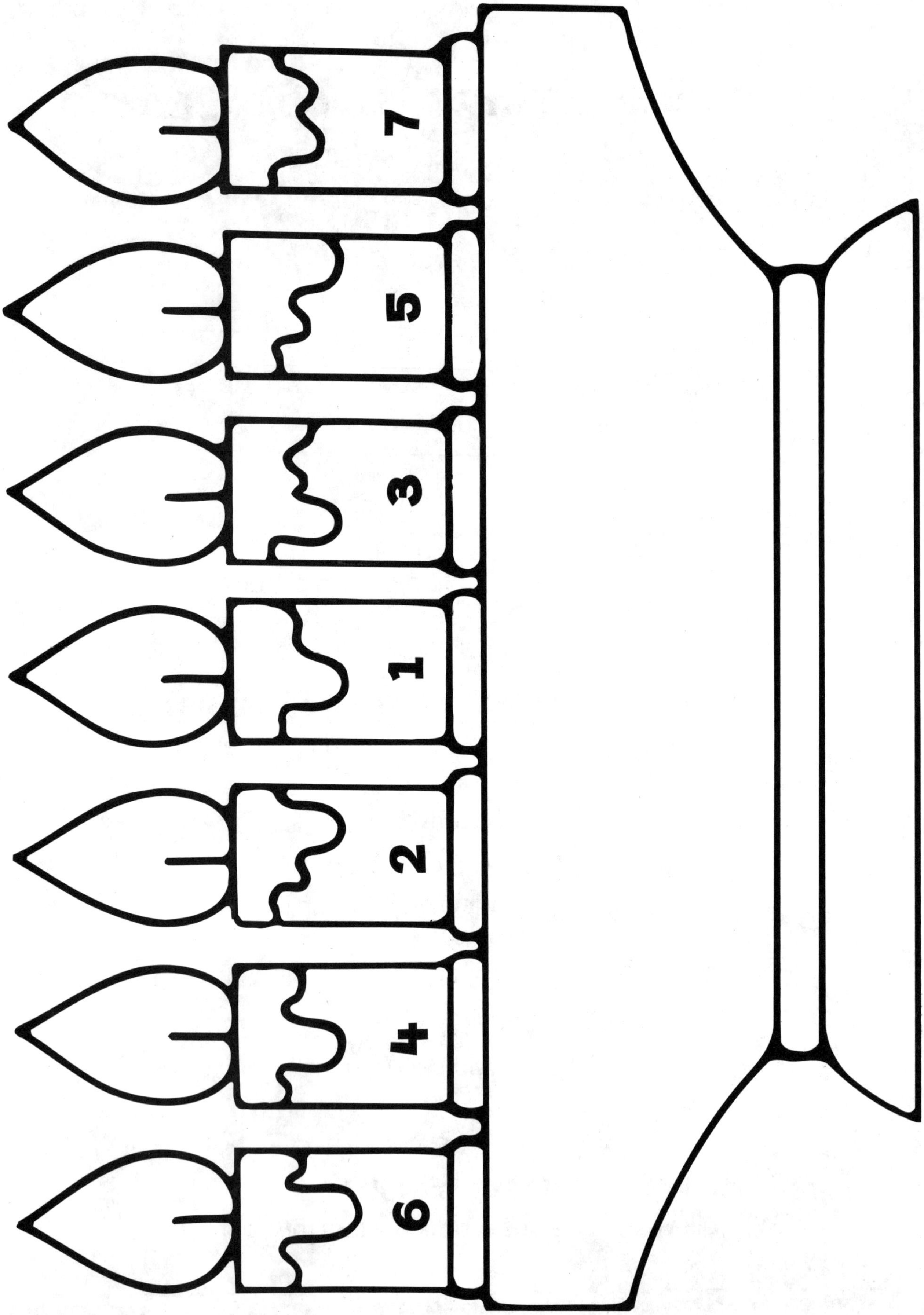
7
5
3
1
2
4
6

PLACE ALONG EDGE
OF PAPER.

AWARDS, INCENTIVES, AND MORE

Getting Started

Make several photocopies of the reproducibles on pages 138 through 142. Giving out the bookmarks, pencil toppers, notes, and certificates will show students your enthusiasm for their efforts and achievements. Plus, bookmarks and pencil toppers are a fun treat for students celebrating birthdays.

- Provide materials for decorating, including markers, color pencils, and stickers.

- Encourage students to bring home their creations to share and celebrate with family members.

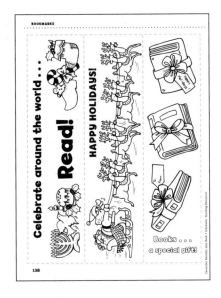

★ BOOKMARKS

1. Photocopy onto tagboard and cut apart.

2. For more fanfare, punch a hole on one end and tie on a length of colorful ribbon or yarn.

★ PENCIL TOPPERS

1. Photocopy onto tagboard and cut out.

2. Use an art knife to cut through the Xs.

3. Slide a pencil through the Xs as shown.

★ SEND-HOME NOTES

1. Photocopy and cut apart.

2. Record the child's name and the date.

3. Add your signature.

4. Add more details about the student's day on the back of the note.

★ CERTIFICATES

1. Photocopy.

2. Record the child's name and other information, as directed.

3. Add details about the child's achievement (if applicable), then add your signature and the date.

Celebrate around the world . . .

Read!

HAPPY HOLIDAYS!

Happy Holidays!

To:
From:

Books . . . a special gift!

December Monthly Idea Book © Scholastic Teaching Resources

_____
Student's Name

did a great job today!

_____   _____
Teacher   Date

_____
Student's Name

was a perfect Santa's helper today!

_____   _____
Teacher   Date

_____
Student's Name

was a wonderful student today!

_____   _____
Teacher   Date

_____
Student's Name

was a real joy in class today!

_____   _____
Teacher   Date

December Monthly Idea Book © Scholastic Teaching Resources

Student of the Week

Name _____

School _____

Date _____

Teacher _____

Certificate of Achievement

presented to

_____
Name

in recognition of _____

_____
Teacher

_____
Date

Hanukkah Word Find, page 73

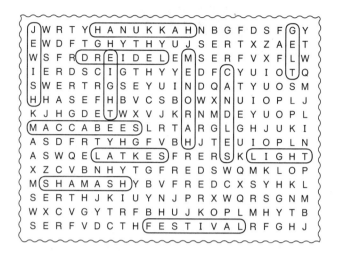

December Monthly Idea Book © Scholastic Teaching Resources

Draw lines to match the Hanukkah facts below:

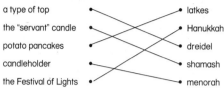

a type of top   latkes
the "servant" candle   Hanukkah
potato pancakes   dreidel
candleholder   shamash
the Festival of Lights   menorah

Countries-Around-the-World Word Find, page 91

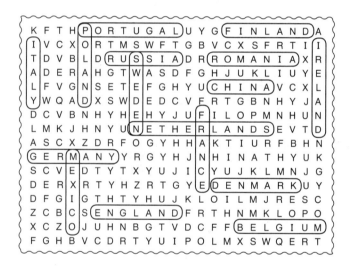

Holiday Word Find, page 100

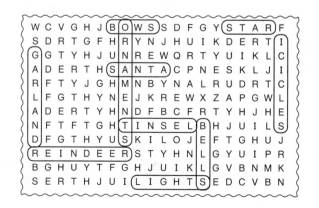

Unscramble the names of Santa's reindeer.
Use the names in the box to help you.

PDIUC   C U P I D
XINVE   V I X E N
ZNETILB   B L I T Z E N
HSREAD   D A S H E R
MOTEC   C O M E T
CANDRE   D A N C E R
DULOHPR   R U D O L P H
CRNEARP   P R A N C E R
DDNORE   D O N D E R

NOTES

December Monthly Idea Book © Scholastic Teaching Resources